BEYOND
LIMITS

BEYOND LIMITS

*Stories of
Third-Trimester
Abortion Care*

Shelley Sella, MD

BEACON PRESS, BOSTON

BEACON PRESS
Boston, Massachusetts
www.beacon.org

Beacon Press books
are published under the auspices of
the Unitarian Universalist Association of Congregations.

28 27 26 25   8 7 6 5 4 3 2 1

This book is printed on acid-free paper that meets the uncoated paper
ANSI/NISO specifications for permanence as revised in 1992.

Text design and composition by Kim Arney

*Library of Congress Cataloging-in-Publication
Data is available for this title.*
ISBN: 978-0-8070-2059-3; e-book: 978-0-8070-2060-9;
audiobook: 978-0-8070-2080-7

*For Dr. George R. Tiller and
Dr. Carmen Landau, mentor and mentee
May their memories be for a blessing.*

CONTENTS

FOREWORD

I have had the privilege of dedicating my medical career to the full spectrum of obstetric and gynecologic care in Alabama for over seventeen years. In that time, I have celebrated new life with thousands of families, guided individuals through the journey of infertility, grieved alongside those facing pregnancy loss, and offered care and counsel to patients navigating the most complex and sometimes emotionally charged decisions of their lives. I have proudly provided abortion care—a vital and deeply personal part of reproductive health that has been under siege in many states for decades.

Providing abortion care has never been just a medical service for me. It is about compassion, autonomy, and advocacy. It is about standing with patients at the most vulnerable crossroads of their lives—whether they are choosing to end an undesired pregnancy, navigating a heartbreaking medical necessity; they are always making a choice that is nuanced and deeply personal. Throughout my career, I've witnessed firsthand the intense stigma and political barriers that abortion providers face. Yet the patients, providers, and advocates in this space are some of the most compassionate, courageous, and dedicated people I have ever known. This is how I met Shelley Sella—through a shared commitment to a fundamental truth: *access to safe, compassionate abortion care is a human right.*

Shelley's journey, as chronicled in *Beyond Limits*, offers an unflinching, intimate look at what it means to answer the call to this kind of work. As a provider of third-trimester abortion care in Albuquerque, Shelley's experiences illuminate the strength, complexity, and compassion required to support patients in the most trying circumstances. Like many of us in this field, Shelley came to this work not out of simple choice but out of personal experience, a commitment to justice, and a desire to ensure that others are met with care and dignity in their most difficult moments.

Beyond Limits is not simply a clinical account. It is a deeply personal exploration of the emotional and moral dimensions of abortion care—the kind of story that challenges the false narratives perpetuated by politics and stigma. Through her work, Shelley provides readers with insight into both the practical and emotional aspects of abortion care—and the real-life consequences of restricting access to it. For many, her story will challenge assumptions about what it means to choose abortion and confront the prejudices that fuel so many laws and public opinions.

One of the great injustices of our time is the way so many have ignored how quickly individual experiences can shift perspectives. Many who claim opposition to abortion find themselves changed when they or someone they love requires this care. Yet this disconnection—this unwillingness to place themselves in another's shoes—has led to the erasure of human stories and the dismantling of a basic right. *Beyond Limits* confronts that disconnection head-on, offering readers a window into the complexity, love, strength, and necessity of reproductive choice.

This book is a reminder of what lawmakers, advocates, and the public alike must grapple with: the profound humanity at the heart of every decision to seek an abortion. For every patient who accessed abortion care and felt relief, for every patient who sought it but was unable to access it, *Beyond Limits* offers our stories. It shares the dignity, the grief, the hope—and the humanity.

If you are someone who has struggled to truly understand what it means to seek, provide, or fight for safe and compassionate abortion care, let this book guide you. It is more than a story of personal experiences; it's a reminder of what is possible when care is grounded in compassion and humanity rather than fear and judgment. Shelley offers readers an invitation: *to see, to listen, and to understand.*

Beyond Limits is both a testament to the strength of abortion providers and a call to empathy, advocacy, and solidarity. Shelley's narrative is one that will resonate with anyone who values autonomy, compassion, and the ability to make decisions free from judgment and interference.

I am so grateful for her courage, her passion, and her voice—and for the way she has chosen to share her story.

May her words inspire change, compassion, and understanding.

—DR. YASHICA ROBINSON
Alabama Women's Center
OB/GYN, Advocate for Reproductive Justice

AUTHOR'S
NOTE

Beyond Limits is about my almost twenty years providing third-trimester abortion care. It draws heavily from my experiences with patients. With the exception of two former patients—one whose name and story appears on anti-abortion websites and another who agreed to use her name—I have changed patients' names and residences and have formed composite true stories to preserve their privacy. The quotations that preface each chapter are either direct patient quotes or quotes that Dr. George R. Tiller shared during our work together, as indicated. He repeated these epigraphs in many forms—in person, in interviews, and in talks at conferences. They came to be known in the wider abortion provider community as "Tillerisms."[1]

The book is divided into two sections. Part 1 weaves the stories of six patients who came for care at the abortion clinic where I practiced with the story of my own life and career. Part 2 addresses commonly asked questions regarding third-trimester abortion care, including: "Why did she wait so long?" and "Why doesn't she just continue the pregnancy and give the baby up for adoption?"

I recognize that not all who are capable of pregnancy identify as women. Today, more abortion patients, and more providers and staff, identify as trans men or nonbinary. However, in *Beyond*

Limits, I largely use *woman* and *patient* to describe those I cared for, along with she/her and they/them pronouns. This reflects the language used in the period in which I practiced. Moreover, it is important to recognize that attacks on abortion are rooted in a patriarchal society that is deeply misogynist. Abortion care would look very different if cisgender men could get pregnant. An egalitarian society would recognize the lifesaving nature of abortion care.

Beyond Limits contains descriptions of abortion and abortion procedures, as well as sexual and domestic violence.

INTRODUCTION

Miscarriage is what happens when your body isn't ready to have a baby. Abortion is what happens when the rest of you isn't.

—ANONYMOUS PATIENT

It's 3:00 a.m. and my thirty-three-year-old patient Clarissa is in labor. She called the clinic half an hour ago to say that she was having contractions, and we instructed her to come in. While waiting for her arrival, her labor support doula Kalin and I set up the labor room: turning down the lights, turning on soft meditative music, and placing a few drops of lavender oil in the aromatherapy diffuser.

Clarissa and her husband, Matt, come in holding hands. When she first walks in, she doesn't appear to be in labor. Her hair is neatly tied back in a ponytail, and her face is relaxed. Suddenly she stops walking and squeezes Matt's hand for the ten-second duration of the contraction. "It's been like this for the past hour," she tells me. "I thought that it would be a good idea to call." I tell her she was right. This seems like early labor, but given that Clarissa has already given birth to two children, the last one only two years ago, it could progress quickly.

I bring them to the labor room, where Kalin greets them, helps Clarissa change into a gown, and gets Matt settled into a chair next to the bed. Clarissa hasn't been sleeping well lately. At first, she lies in bed, eyes closed, moaning with contractions that occur every seven to ten minutes. Gradually, the contractions become more intense, and Clarissa is increasingly uncomfortable. She gets out of bed and walks around the room, one arm draped over Matt, the other over me, while Kalin croons softly, "You are doing so well. Your body is working perfectly. You are so strong."

The contractions are now getting stronger, lasting longer and coming more frequently. Clarissa is working harder. Her face is flushed. Her ponytail has loosened, and hair covers her eyes. She stops walking and tries bouncing on the big orange birthing ball that's in the room, but she cannot get comfortable.

"I feel like I have to push," she moans.

"That's good," I respond. "Let me check you."

Getting back in bed seems too challenging right now. Clarissa drops down onto a black yoga mat in the corner of the room. Matt sits behind her and she leans against him while Kalin squats by her side; both are supporting her. I check her cervix and let her know that the baby, who they already named Jeremiah, is coming.

Jeremiah is out in two pushes. As Clarissa and Matt had previously requested, I immediately place him on Clarissa's chest, and she hugs him tightly. Matt gazes at Jeremiah over Clarissa's shoulders. The baby is not crying, but his parents are. Last week, Jeremiah, their longed-for child, was diagnosed with a massive stroke in the womb with no possibility of recovery. Clarissa has just had a twenty-eight-week abortion at Southwestern Women's Options clinic in Albuquerque, New Mexico.

I was the first woman doctor in the United States to openly provide abortions in the third trimester of pregnancy, the period from twenty-four to twenty-six weeks until term at forty weeks.[1] When I began in 2002, there were only three doctors doing this work. Currently, there are about ten. For twenty years, I traveled from my home in Oakland, California, to other states to provide the type of abortion that is condemned by so many and still only available in three states. Through spending time with patients, listening to their stories, and learning about the difficult circumstances that drove them to seek a third-trimester abortion, I came to understand that even though this procedure makes up a small segment of abortion care, it is vitally important.[2] I felt compelled to continue to offer this service and to train others to follow in my footsteps. I initially worked in Wichita, Kansas, where I was mentored and trained by Dr. George Tiller at his clinic. I continued to do this work in Albuquerque, New Mexico, even after Dr. Tiller was assassinated at his church by an anti-abortion extremist in 2009.

I started keeping a journal my first week of training with Dr. Tiller in 2002 and continued through 2021, when I finally stepped away from practicing. I didn't know when I began that two decades down the road, *Roe v. Wade* would be overturned and that most or all abortion care would soon become illegal in many states. As of this writing, thirteen states have completely banned abortion and eight more have restricted it more severely than the standards set by the *Roe v. Wade* decision.

Looking back, I'm grateful to have taken such care to preserve these patients' stories and my experiences caring for them so I can share the lessons I learned. The most important is this: understanding the lives and circumstances of those seeking third-trimester abortion care is essential. Without this context, it is difficult to imagine why someone might need a third-trimester abortion, and without context, the procedure itself is easy to vilify and malign.

VIABILITY

The *Roe* decision of 1973 legalized abortion throughout the US. In that decision, the Supreme Court said that once a pregnancy was viable, a state could restrict or ban abortion except when necessary to preserve the life or health of the mother.[3] *Roe* was overturned in 2022 in the *Dobbs v. Jackson* decision, leaving each state able to make its own laws and regulations regarding abortion. Some states have banned abortion entirely, and many others have imposed limits. Just a handful of states—Alaska, Colorado, Maryland, New Jersey, New Mexico, Oregon, and Vermont—and the District of Columbia have not prohibited post-viable abortions.

But what is viability? In the *Roe* decision, the fetus is said to be viable when it is "potentially able to live outside the mother's womb, albeit with artificial aid."[4] *Roe* and subsequent decisions acknowledge, however, that there is no bright line, no fixed gestational age when viability can be assigned. The 1976 *Planned Parenthood of Central Missouri v. Danforth* decision states

> that it is not the proper function of the legislature or the courts to place viability, which essentially is a medical concept, at a specific point in the gestation period. The time when viability is achieved may vary with each pregnancy, and the determination of whether a particular fetus is viable is, and must be, a matter for the judgment of the responsible attending physician.[5]

Despite this acknowledgment of the variability of when a fetus may be able to survive outside the womb, that point was commonly considered to be twenty-eight weeks in 1973, while today, due to advances in medical care, it is considered to be twenty-three to twenty-four weeks, with some cases of survival at twenty-two weeks. Most of the third-trimester abortions that I performed were between twenty-seven and twenty-nine weeks.

For the courts, viability is thought of in terms of potential survival, without consideration of the short- and long-term effects of survival on the baby and the family. In practice, babies that survive delivery at twenty-three to twenty-four weeks have a mortality rate as high as 44 percent and often suffer from profound medical complications, including long-lasting brain, heart, and lung damage.

As a doctor, I do not rely on a supposedly objective standard of viability. Rather, I have come to view viability more holistically. Every patient who comes to me for an abortion has considered all the factors relevant to their well-being and to their unborn child's and concluded that this particular pregnancy is nonviable. This decision is based on both the external circumstances of their life and their internal understanding of those circumstances.

Factors that my patients consider—and it is often a confluence of many—include their own health and safety, their baby's future health and safety, financial resources, the family's ability to access the level of healthcare the baby will require, adequate food and shelter, their age and level of maturity, educational and occupational opportunities, and family and community support and love. Perhaps their decisions would be different if they lived in a country with universal healthcare, a country that guaranteed a living income and provided affordable housing and childcare, but that is not the country they live in. Patients make their decisions based on the reality of their lives, not the fantasy version of their lives. This understanding framed my work and allowed me to perform abortions in all trimesters with a sense of commitment and the knowledge that I was responding to my patients' needs.[6]

Third-trimester abortions are rare, but the situations that drive women to seek them are not. What really differentiates third-trimester patients from those in the first and second trimesters is the degree of desperation they feel. These patients know that if I am unable to care for them, they will be forced to continue the pregnancy and they and their child will suffer its consequences. They will be forced to bear the increased risks of childbirth over abortion. *The Turnaway Study*, the landmark longitudinal research study that compares outcomes of women who had an abortion to those who were turned away from abortion clinics because they were too far along in their pregnancies, shows that those forced to continue their pregnancies had increased rates of poverty and abuse compared to those able to access an abortion.[7] They were more likely to experience severe health complications at the end of their pregnancies and physical health issues even years afterward. My patients know these risks well without having read the study. The fear that accompanies their realization that our clinic is the last resort for them can be overwhelming. I've seen those feelings on their faces and heard them in the words of my patients when we first meet. More than one patient has told me that condemning her to give birth would be a death sentence and that an abortion would be lifesaving.

When third-trimester abortion is in the news, it most commonly regards women who receive a late diagnosis of a lethal or severe fetal anomaly or those with late-developing medical conditions whose lives would be at risk if they continued the pregnancy. Those with a fetal anomaly would be forced to deliver a child whose life, however short, would be one of suffering.

Patients whose babies have a fetal anomaly who come to the clinic for a third-trimester abortion receive desperately needed emotional care in a peaceful environment where their wishes are respected. All the patients who come to the clinic are there for the same reason, and the staff are caring and highly skilled in supporting patients and families who have come to end a pregnancy.

But patients whose babies have fetal anomalies are not the only patients who seek third-trimester abortions. I have also cared for victims of domestic violence who were trapped in their home and couldn't escape to seek an abortion until their abuser was jailed. I've cared for women who were raped and were so traumatized that they could not confront the possibility of pregnancy. I have performed abortions for women whose birth control, even the most effective kinds, failed. Because they were on birth control, they could not believe that their bodily changes were pregnancy related until they finally discovered that they were pregnant and in the third trimester.

I have assisted mothers who were initially planning to continue the pregnancy but lost their jobs and could barely afford to care for the children they already had. I have also cared for many teenagers and even younger girls who were too afraid to tell anyone that they were pregnant and who hid behind baggy clothes until they could no longer keep their pregnancy a secret. And in recent years, I saw more and more women who *did* seek abortions earlier in pregnancy, but the barriers of different state regulations regarding gestational age bans, waiting periods, cost, transportation, and increased demand due to clinics around the country being forced to close had prevented them from obtaining one until they managed to make their way to my door. What these barriers failed to do, however, was to dissuade women from ending their pregnancy.

All these women and girls deserved to have a safe and legal abortion, and, thankfully, they did. They each had a story to tell. They explained to me what compelled them to seek a third-trimester abortion despite all the barriers, hurdles, and stigma they faced. Many of them initially held strong anti-abortion views while simultaneously believing that having an abortion was absolutely essential to prevent suffering for themselves and their families. Many also expressed deep concern for their unborn child. If they were to give birth, they all wanted their child to live a good life, with adequate food, shelter, and opportunities. They knew, to their deepest core, that the circumstances of their particular pregnancy would make that impossible. I fully embraced my patients' hopes, dreams, and aspirations for themselves and their families. I was proud to be able to provide them with care that could make that possible.

A third-trimester pregnancy is not "a clump of cells." It is not "tissue." Although until birth it is technically a fetus, most would consider a third-trimester pregnancy a baby, and if it were born alive, it *would* be a baby. It is the understandable discomfort surrounding "babyhood" that many feel—even those who consider themselves pro-choice, and even some doctors who provide abortion care earlier in pregnancy—that contributes to the taboo surrounding abortions later in pregnancy. I have learned in my many years in practice that doctors, patients, and advocates can have conflicting and complex feelings about abortion. But providing this care has also convinced me that no one can walk in someone else's shoes. My job is to set aside judgments, listen deeply, and support patients as they navigate what can be a difficult and painful decision-making process.

Understanding third-trimester abortions is the key to understanding all abortion care. If we can open our hearts to the most desperate among us, we can understand all who seek to have an abortion. We can understand the importance of safe, legal, and accessible abortion care for all, during all trimesters of pregnancy.

I believe that now is the time to reevaluate what it means to be pro-choice. If we are fully committed to supporting women's decisions, we must eliminate all barriers to accessing abortion care. There is no choice to be had if abortion, at all stages of pregnancy, is not accessible. We must realize that gestational limit are arbitrary and do not reflect the reality of women's lives. We must understand that accepting *any* gestational limits is a slippery slope to the total bans we are seeing in increasing numbers of states. And we must wholeheartedly support the growing number of women who are driven to seek a third-trimester abortion who are as deserving as anyone else of compassionate and competent care.

A father of a gravely ill unborn child once told me that, in light of his child's condition, he considered it immoral to *continue* the pregnancy. A young rape victim's mother once said to me, "You don't know the story until you are the story." My hope is that by sharing my story and the stories of the patients I cared for, many more people will come to understand third-trimester abortion in a new way and will thus have greater understanding of, and compassion for, those who desperately need such care.

BEYOND
LIMITS

PART ONE

CHAPTER I

Tuesday Morning, Fetal Indications

I am a Catholic, and I am not happy about the situation.
But God gave us the ability to think, and for us to use
our judgment and especially to be our own person, and
I feel that I did this to help out the child and me.

—ANONYMOUS PATIENT

Today is Tuesday, and Mary is crying. My Tuesday patients are usually in tears when we first meet. Tuesday is when I start the week's third-trimester abortions for patients who have made the careful decision to have an abortion late in pregnancy. A third-trimester abortion is a multiday process, and it's often emotional—for the patients, for their partners or parents, and for me and the clinic staff.

I'm sitting in front of Mary and her husband, Christopher. I cross my legs, and my purple scrubs hike up slightly, revealing the top of today's cheerful socks: baby sea turtles waddling toward the ocean. "I'm sorry you had to come here," I tell the couple. Christopher is gripping his wife's slight shoulders and seems almost angry. His whole face is darkened by his frown.

"I'm sorry your baby is sick," I say gently. "And I'm sorry you couldn't be cared for in your hometown. I know this is the last place you would ever want to be."

Mary and this week's five other third-trimester patients had to travel out of state to Southwestern Women's Options in

Albuquerque, one of the very few clinics in the United States performing abortions in all trimesters—first, second, and third. This week, my patients come from Missouri, Arkansas, Texas, Florida, and Ohio. Three of them are being seen for fetal indications, which means they are ending the pregnancy because of severe fetal anomalies. The other three are here for maternal indications, due to severe challenges in their or their families' lives.

Each patient's journey began when they called the clinic and spoke to our phone counselor for an intake and explanation of the third-trimester procedure. She explained that it starts on Tuesday, with the administration of a medication to stop the fetal heartbeat and the preparation of the cervix. When the cervix is ready, which may take several days, labor is induced, and the patient delivers a stillborn. The counselor also always warns patients: "I want you to know that there will be protestors as you come in. They are not allowed to come onto our property. Please ignore them."

Despite this, patients are still taken aback. When they and their companions drove in earlier this morning, they had to pass a handful of protestors on the strip of public property at the far edge of the parking lot. The protestors carry the same mass-produced signs seen at so many abortion clinics across the country: "Abortion is murder," "Abortion stops a heartbeat," and "Pray to end abortion." After so many years, I am mostly inured to these protestors, to their signs and their insults. They yell, "Shelley, go back to California." They never call me "Dr. Sella," as they refuse to pay me any respect. I ignore them, but I am still angered that patients are subjected to their vitriol. Sometimes I want to scream obscenities at them, but I know that is exactly the response the protestors want, so instead, I curse them under my breath as I drive past.

At times our patients enter the clinic angry and upset. They mistakenly believe that if only the protestors knew *their* situation, they would understand and not harass them. I know by now that this is not true, especially given how many of my patients have told me that they strongly opposed abortion until they needed one themselves.

In contrast to the ugliness outside, the patients enter a waiting room that is bright, airy, and peaceful, with large windows and big, healthy plants, thanks to our green-thumbed phone counselor, Belinda.* Patients fill out paperwork, then get blood work and an ultrasound to confirm gestational age before meeting with a counselor. The role of the counselor is crucial. She reviews the procedure with patients and answers their questions. Importantly, she starts to relieve the patients' anxiety, something I continue to do when we meet. For many patients in the third trimester, this will be the first time they have talked to anyone about their current situation and about making a decision that for some is difficult and for others is clear and straightforward. The counselor lets her patients know that this clinic is a safe place. Within these walls, there is no judgment, only compassion. We are here to care for our patients.

Before I enter the room to meet the week's patients, I check with the counselor to see whether there are any specific issues or concerns that I should address. We start with the week's fetal-indication patients: There is Mary, along with two others, Jamie and Amrita. Jamie's baby has hypoplastic left heart syndrome, a serious heart defect that is lethal if untreated. Amrita's has lissen-cephaly, a very rare, severe brain anomaly. And Mary's baby has a meningomyelocele with Arnold-Chiari malformation, a severe neural tube defect. I meet with Mary first.

MARY AND CHRISTOPHER

Mary, forty-seven, and Christopher, forty-nine, are a white couple from Missouri. They met when she was in her late thirties. By the time they felt ready to have children, she was in her early forties and could not get pregnant without medical intervention. She began rounds of in vitro fertilization (IVF) and was thrilled to find herself pregnant on the fourth attempt. She and Christopher

---

*Abby, Belinda, Delia, Flora, Margaret, and Reyna are pseudonyms for staff members. All other names of non-patients are real, unless otherwise indicated.

had taken out loans to pay for the IVF, an expensive procedure that wasn't covered by their insurance, and another attempt might not be possible. How amazing to find out that she was finally pregnant! Throughout the pregnancy, Mary's joy was tempered by anxiety she tried to keep in check. Her greatest fear was that she would miscarry and lose the pregnancy. Perhaps because of this fear, she reveled in all the sensations of pregnancy, even some quite severe first-trimester nausea and vomiting. By the second trimester, she was feeling well and was enjoying looking down at her ever-expanding belly. She began to feel confident in her body's ability to carry a pregnancy. She felt good! And then, after a call from her doctor's office, she didn't.

An abnormal test result and further testing revealed that her baby had a neural tube defect, a meningomyelocele with Arnold-Chiari malformation. This is not a lethal anomaly, however. Unless they ended the pregnancy, their baby would live.

Mary and Christopher began to educate themselves about this neural tube defect and the possibilities for treatment. They sought a second, then a third, opinion and even had a consultation at a medical center offering maternal-fetal surgery before coming to a decision.

A meningomyelocele occurs when there is an opening in the part of the neural tube that goes on to form the spinal column. This opening can be small or large, and it allows the spinal cord and its associated nervous tissue to herniate, or poke through, resulting in tissue outside the spinal column being exposed to amniotic fluid rather than protected on the inside. The longer the exposure to amniotic fluid, the more severe the injury. And the higher the defect in the spine, the worse the injury. Almost 50 percent of the time—and in Mary's case—the meningomyelocele occurs in the lower spine, affecting the lumbar and sacral areas. Depending on its severity, this defect causes inability to control the bladder and the bowel, as well as paraplegia, which is the loss of sensation and movement of the legs and feet.

Meningomyelocele is often accompanied by a brain anomaly called Arnold-Chiari malformation, which is the case for Mary's baby, and it greatly impacts the child's quality of life. In this situation, part of the brain herniates down into the spinal canal, distorting the brain's anatomy and affecting its function. The normal flow of the cerebrospinal fluid that surrounds the brain and spinal cord is blocked, leading to fluid buildup, which is called hydrocephalous. If severe, hydrocephalous compresses normal brain tissue and leads to major intellectual disability and death. When hydrocephalous is present, a surgical shunt must be placed after birth to divert cerebrospinal fluid to the abdominal cavity. Not uncommonly, the shunt itself becomes blocked or infected, requiring hospitalizations to replace the shunt and treat the infection.

If Mary were to continue the pregnancy, most typically the baby would have surgery within forty-eight hours of birth to close the defect and place a shunt. A newer, more complicated surgery can sometimes be done prior to birth, while the baby is still in the womb, to try to prevent ongoing damage. If Mary qualified for this maternal-fetal surgery—and, interestingly, it is commonly referred to as fetal surgery, completely negating the role of and risks to the mother—both she and the baby would undergo major surgery with the possibility of serious complications for each of them.

What Mary and Christopher came to realize was that there is no cure. Surgery may stop the degeneration of the nervous system, but it cannot reverse it, and looking at surgical outcomes is just one factor to consider. A "successful" postnatal surgery means that 80 percent of children will still have hydrocephalous, requiring placement of a shunt, with lifelong monitoring for blockage and infection, and almost half will have to use a wheelchair. They could expect to care for a child with special needs who might not walk and might not have bowel or bladder function. Given the associated hydrocephalous, their child could also have significant intellectual disabilities. The question Mary and Christopher needed to answer, through their research and follow-up consultations, was whether they could handle the special needs of their baby. And this question, for Mary and Christopher and all parents confronting prenatal diagnoses, soon became a painful string of questions, exacerbated by the fact that they live in a country whose social policies express love for the disabled fetus but offer little support to the disabled child and family.

Patients wonder whether they can afford to care for a child with special needs—not just the costs of the immediate surgery and hospitalization, but also subsequent surgeries if required. Rarely does insurance, for those who have it, cover 100 percent of all costs, and co-pays can be astronomical. Most insurance in the United States is employer based. Would they be able to hold on to a job while providing the care a child with special needs requires? For those on Medicaid, would it cover all the costs associated with the care of a disabled child? And they worry about the costs of accessible housing for a child who uses a wheelchair.

It is not only costs that parents consider when coming to a decision. They wonder: What will be the impact of hospitalizations, not just on their child's health but also on their social and emotional development? What resources are available in their community for children with special needs? What educational opportunities are there?

How will they be able to maintain a healthy relationship with each other when so much of their time is focused on caring for this child? In the face of the stress of caring for a child with special needs, how will they maintain their own mental health, as well as their family's? Who will care for this child when they are no longer alive? And if this is their only child, will the child then be institutionalized?

All these questions underlie the most important questions of all: What will be our child's quality of life? Will our child suffer?

The answers to these questions, in consultation with medical providers, family, friends, and spiritual leaders, are what lead some parents to seek an abortion for their unborn child with an anomaly.

In Mary and Christopher's case, they learned that the meningomyelocele was large and the hydrocephalous was severe. They considered all their options. Surgery could improve, but not cure, these abnormalities. By now they both were already in their late forties and still had elderly parents who needed their care. They could not imagine how they could also care for a child with special needs. They also wondered what would happen as they themselves aged. Their decision was not based on religion, despite being practicing Catholics, nor was it based on politics. It was made after the careful consideration of multiple factors, one interweaving with the next. In the end, Mary and Christopher were clear about one thing: as long or as short as their child's life might be, they did not want their child to suffer.

Mary's presence at the clinic is especially poignant. For women like Mary who have been through the difficult process of artificial reproductive technology, it is particularly heartbreaking to finally achieve pregnancy only to find out that the baby has severe anomalies. This may be Mary's last chance to conceive. Mary and Christopher came to the decision to end this pregnancy only after extreme deliberation and with great sadness.

Like many of my patients, Mary and her husband are religious. And like many of my patients, they're also anti-abortion. "I have theological issues with abortion," Christopher tells me. But after extensive prenatal testing, their baby's prognosis is grim. And given their ages, they worry that their severely disabled child will have no one to care for him once they are no longer alive.

When patients' religious beliefs conflict with abortion, the pain, distress, and anxiety about having an abortion in the third trimester intensify. Mary's anxiety was evident from her first call to our clinic. She asked the phone counselor the same questions over and over. In a first, she asked for my age, seeking reassurance that an older, experienced doctor would be caring for her.

When I see her, Mary's concerns are still evident. She asks me: "Will I be able to have children in the future?" It is a question within a question. The first question is, will abortion cause me to be infertile, a common anti-abortion myth. The deeper question is, as I interpret it, will I be okay? Will I be able to live my life fully and realize my hopes and dreams?

Though I reassure Mary that the risk of a complication is rare, I don't sugarcoat her predicament. The likelihood that this abortion will prevent her from conceiving in the future is small, but based on my years as an ob-gyn, I tell her that, given her age and that this pregnancy was IVF-conceived, the likelihood of her conceiving in the future is also small. This is both sad and sobering, but as her doctor, I must tell her. Mary has no other questions.

Christopher, in contrast, has a lot to say. He is a deeply religious Catholic, someone who takes his faith seriously and tries to live by its edicts. We do not discuss the Catholic Church's prohibition on IVF and how he reconciles that with Mary's conception. But Christopher is affronted by the idea of the injection that will stop the fetal heartbeat. He compares it to a heart attack and says, "It would be painful if I had one." I wonder whether he got this idea from an anti-abortion website.

"I don't believe so," I respond. "It's a gradual slowing of the heart, until it stops."

I feel sad for Mary and Christopher, as I can see how their desire to spare their child a lifetime of suffering conflicts with their religious beliefs. I hope that this initial conversation affords them some relief.

I tell Mary and Christopher that, as of now, *Mary* is my patient. Until her arrival at our clinic, there were two patients, Mary and her baby. And increasingly, both legally and societally, the idea that the fetus takes precedence over the woman is gaining ground. However, now that Mary has made the decision to end the pregnancy, *she* is the only patient. It is now her health and safety, both physical and emotional, that is my primary concern. This reality can be a hard concept to accept because it acknowledges that this pregnancy is going to end without a baby. Yet it is also a relief for them to know that all of our focus is on ensuring Mary's health and safety.

By this point, Mary seems a little less anxious, Christopher a little less tense. I review the consent forms that they have already gone over with the counselor, and we sign them. It is a moment of affirmation. I affirm that I will care for Mary to the best of my ability and Mary affirms that she trusts me to do so. I hand Mary a copy of the book I give to all fetal-indication patients, *A Time to*

Decide, a Time to Heal: For Parents Making Difficult Decisions About Babies They Love.[1]

"It's for people like you," I say, "people who are ending the pregnancy because there's something wrong." I ask Mary what she's been calling the being inside her. "Baby," she says, like most fetal-indication patients. (I do not ask this question of maternal-indication patients, preferring to take my cues from them. If they say *baby*, I say *baby*, and if they say *fetus*, so do I.) Sometimes, fetal-indication patients seem almost embarrassed when they say *baby*, as if it's not okay to describe what others call a fetus a baby. And, sometimes tearily and sometimes proudly, they tell me their baby's name.

"You know, women end their pregnancies for many reasons," I tell Mary and Christopher, "but you wouldn't be here if your baby was healthy. In the book, people describe what it's been like for them to go through this process. I would like to give this to you." On the first page above the title, I write the date, and below it I inscribe:

To Mary and Christopher,
In the spirit of healing,
Dr. Sella

I tell them that in the afternoon, there will be an information and support group for them and the other two couples who are ending their pregnancies because their baby is unhealthy. We'll be able to talk more then, and the families will be able to talk with one another.

I leave the room. Momentarily, a counselor will escort Christopher to the waiting room and take Mary to a procedure room, to begin preparing her cervix and to proceed with the fetal injection.

JAMIE AND ROBERT

In the adjoining room I meet Jamie and Robert, a white couple in their early thirties from a small town in Arkansas. They both have the skinny, jittery look of longtime cigarette smokers. They tell me they are barely scraping by, supporting themselves and their four-year-old son on Robert's salary as a car mechanic and Jamie's as a part-time worker at a fast-food restaurant. Their pregnancy was unintended, but it was joyfully accepted. Then Jamie was shocked to learn that her baby had a serious heart defect, hypoplastic left heart syndrome (HLHS).

While neural tube defects represent one category of anomalies that can result in lifelong intellectual and physical disabilities, heart defects represent another type that present different considerations for parents. HLHS represents 7 to 9 percent of all congenital heart defects and is the most common heart defect I see in my practice. It includes a large group of cardiac anomalies, not all of which are present in each individual situation. The most prominent feature is that the left ventricle, the largest chamber of the heart and the one that pumps oxygenated blood to the whole body, is undeveloped and nonfunctional.

There is no cure, and the condition is fatal if left untreated. But treatment is complex, reconfiguring the heart so that it can take over the function of the left ventricle. It requires three successive surgeries over a period of up to four years at a major medical center that can perform pediatric cardiac surgery. The first surgery is done within the first week of life and has a 16 percent mortality rate during the hospitalization. Those babies that survive and go home have a 10 to 15 percent mortality rate and require intense surveillance until the next surgery. The second surgery occurs at three to six months. The last surgery occurs between eighteen months and four years. Success rates have increased over the years, but by the time they are twenty years old, one out of three of these children will die. Those that survive are at risk for major medical complications, and almost one in ten will require a heart transplant.

To continue a pregnancy with HLHS and to navigate all the surgeries, procedures, hospitalizations, and home care that are required is a major commitment of time and resources for an uncertain outcome. This diagnosis ultimately compelled Jamie to decide to end her pregnancy. But making the decision to end the pregnancy took time and deliberation.

When Jamie first got the diagnosis, she hoped it was an error, but advanced testing and consultations with pediatric cardiologists confirmed it. Jamie and Robert live in a small town, while the specialist's practice is hours away. It took time to schedule appointments and to make the arrangements to keep the appointments. Jamie had to take time off from work and arrange childcare for their four-year-old. None of this could happen quickly.

If they wanted to continue the pregnancy, they soon realized that these appointments were just the beginning. They would need to drastically transform their lives. Could they uproot themselves and relocate close to a major medical center? Where would they live? How could they support themselves? How could they provide the close surveillance that this baby would need in between surgeries? If they were to spend all their time and energy caring for the needs of this child, how would they care for their other child? And, after they were no longer living, would it be fair to put the responsibility of caring for the complex health needs of this child on their oldest child?

For them, as with Mary and Christopher, these were the important questions: Will my child suffer? How much will my child suffer? And what will be the outcome after all this suffering? Ultimately, Jamie and Robert felt that they had no choice.

They tell me that they are devout churchgoers, deeply religious Pentecostal Christians, and I expect another pained, deeply conflicted couple explaining to me that while they are anti-abortion, they need one. But it doesn't go that way. And once again, I'm reminded not to make assumptions or judge patients based on religion and politics.

They are members of a church in which the pastor really gets into it and jumps ecstatically in front of the congregation. Jamie and Robert prayed and prayed when they got the diagnosis. Finally, they went to their pastor for counsel. He advised them to get a second opinion, and when it confirmed the first, he gave his blessing. God was with them, he said, because Jamie's life was paramount.

I've heard similar stories from other patients who had talked to their religious leader about their decision, expecting condemnation and instead finding support. What astonishes me, though, is the next part of the story. The congregation was told about the abortion and supported Jamie and Robert. Together, they raised enough money for the couple to rent a car to drive to the clinic.

Suddenly, I understand why, although they are deeply distressed, their level of anxiety is considerably lower than that of Mary and Christopher. Surrounded by support from their pastor and their community, Jamie and Robert can focus on the loss of their child. Meanwhile, Mary and Christopher's grief is overlaid with the guilt that they are going *against* their community and violating one of their most fundamental religious precepts.

AMRITA AND ARUN

Lastly, I meet Amrita and Arun, a couple from India who are living in Texas. They are in their late twenties with a two-year-old. Theirs was a planned and highly desired pregnancy, and they both felt that now was the perfect time to welcome a second child into their family.

However, a routine ultrasound in the second trimester showed brain anomalies, which were confirmed by a subsequent fetal MRI. The testing revealed lissencephaly, or "smooth brain," a condition in which the brain does not have its normal folds. Lissencephaly is associated with intractable seizures and severe developmental delays. Although the average life expectancy is ten years, most children do not progress beyond three-to-five-month-old developmental milestones.

Amrita and Arun were devastated by this news. Amrita tells me that when they learned how rare this anomaly is—approximately one in one hundred thousand births—her first thought was "It's like we won the lottery, only we have bad luck."

The dismal prognosis for this child's short life was intolerable. Continuing the pregnancy was not an option for them, and they sought an abortion in Texas. They were perplexed that, especially given their child's prognosis, it was denied to them, and they would have to leave their state for care.

Over the years, I cared for many Indian patients, and they often shared this puzzlement. Abortion in India is not the political and social hot button issue that it is in the United States, and it is not stigmatized or hidden. Amrita and Arun were open with both sets of parents about their decision and had their unconditional support. In fact, Amrita's mother flew to Texas from India to care for their two-year-old so that they could come to Albuquerque for the abortion.

As I speak with the couple, the only significant question they have is about the possibility of cremation. I tell them they can arrange it through a local funeral home and that it's something we will discuss further that afternoon in the support group meeting.

THE TECHNICAL PREPARATION: TUESDAY MORNING

After I have met with each of my fetal-indication patients, I start the technical part of the abortion, preparing the cervix to dilate and administering the injection that will slow and stop the fetus's heartbeat.

The counselor has escorted each patient to their procedure room, and she steps out while the patient undresses. She returns with a nurse, who administers small doses of a medication to relieve anxiety and a medication to relieve pain through an IV. Once the patient is comfortable on the exam table, the counselor steps out of the room to flip the plastic flag outside the door to red, a signal for me to enter. The lights are dimmed. There is calming music; my patients often say it sounds like they're at a spa. A mobile of a dancing woman hangs over the table.

At the head of the table, the counselor speaks softly to the patient. Quietly, I enter the room with the ultrasound nurse, careful not to disrupt the calm atmosphere. After placing the speculum, the instrument that helps open the vagina, I numb the cervix with a local anesthetic. Under ultrasound guidance, through the vagina, I inject a medication called digoxin, which will stop the fetus's heartbeat in about two to four hours. When it's her turn, Mary asks the counselor to say a prayer with her right before the injection. I recognize the power of these moments. There is no turning back.

After the injection, I place laminaria, small sterile dilators made of seaweed or a synthetic analogue, in the cervix to gradually widen its opening, along with two pieces of gauze to help hold them in place. I remove the speculum and go to the head of the exam table to talk with the patient. Based on my initial assessment of the cervix of each of the three fetal-indication patients, I explain next steps, though I won't know the plan for certain until each returns tomorrow and I recheck her cervix. For Jamie and Amrita, who have given birth before, I plan to start the induction of labor tomorrow. For Mary, who has never delivered, I will reinsert laminaria to continue dilating her cervix. I answer any questions they may have and reassure them that all has gone well and that the recovery room nurse will review everything with them again before they leave. After I leave the room, the counselor helps the patient, who often feels a little nauseated and crampy, to get dressed and head to the recovery room.

The recovery room is large, with recliners for patients to rest on. By each recliner is a small table with a notebook for patients to write their thoughts and to share with the next person who sits there. The notebooks are a written source of support for patients. They are filled with pleas to God and words of encouragement. They help patients realize that they are not alone—that others have gone through this experience and know how they are feeling.

Dear God, please forgive me. I'm not in a good position to have a baby. I know I made the right choice. No regret.

May God forgive us all for we are humans. We fall short sometimes.

Forget about debating the right or wrong of your situation. You made the best choice you could. If you're thanking god, thank him for the opportunity that you have to decide what you want.

You are not stupid or anything like that for getting pregnant. Nor are you a bad person for making this choice. Always do what's right for YOU. Take care of yourself. Don't worry about what people might say. You are going to be okay.

There are many tissue boxes in the room. The nurse provides soda and crackers. She reviews instructions with each patient and lets them know that the on-call phone counselor will call her every evening to check in. After half an hour, the nurse escorts the patients to the waiting room and reminds them to return to the clinic for the afternoon group session with the other fetal-indication patients.

These afternoon groups, just like the recovery room notebooks and the entire setup of the clinic, are designed to offer continued emotional support. This support is an essential aspect of the care that I offer, which I believe all patients deserve.

It is also the kind of support I wish I'd had when I was a scared young teenager.

CHAPTER 2

New York: 1960s–1970s

Everybody needs a little
help every once in a while.

—GEORGE R. TILLER, MD

My mother, Aviva, was born and raised in what was then Palestine and later became the State of Israel. My father, Emanuel, was
born in Poland but managed to escape to Palestine in 1939, right
before the start of World War II. However, Israel of the 1950s
and 1960s was too small for my father's ambitions and too provin-
cial for my mother's romantic dreams of a good life. Instead, they
moved to New York City to raise their four children: my two older
brothers, me, and my younger sister.

In their new country, my father's business became a success.
Yet despite becoming happily rooted in New York, they were still
immigrants, unmoored from family support. Nearly all my father's
family had died in the Holocaust, and my mother's family remained
in Israel. Even as their prospects blossomed, their isolation played
out in our home.

I grew up in an unhappy household. My brothers and I fought
constantly. More accurately, my brothers hit me, and I either tried
to defend myself or locked myself in the bathroom. I was often
chastised by my parents for crying and yelling for help. In Hebrew,
my father would say that I sounded like "a lady in the market"—to
him, a very undesirable character. Years later, one of my mother's
friends told me that, on our family trips to Israel, she noticed how

much and how often my brothers hit me and that Aviva never defended me. Once she asked Aviva about this, and my mother responded that she thought parents should not get involved in their children's conflicts. That might have been a philosophical decision, or it may have been a way for her to cope in a foreign country, away from her own family support and without the wherewithal to ask for help. She was cool and detached. My father was warmer, at times fiery, which made for a volatile relationship between them.

When I was twelve years old, my oldest brother, E., began to abuse me. I will never forget the fear, terror, confusion, and loneliness of this time period. I was the victim of incest from the ages of twelve to fifteen. I was a naïve twelve-year-old, and at first I had no idea what was going on. It never occurred to me to tell my parents, and there was no extended family nearby to turn to. My mother had never intervened to stop my brothers' physical violence, and I never perceived her as someone who would protect me. I understood that my mother was not someone I could turn to when I needed support or help. I also couldn't turn to my father. In the world of the traditional bourgeois white household of the 1950s and '60s, the man earned the salary and the woman was responsible for the home. With that model in place, providing enough money to support the household was his problem; misbehaving children were hers. Meanwhile, despite the abuse, I felt protective of my brother. He was starting to get into trouble and had run away for a time, and family conflict was at an all-time high.

Instead of using my mouth to speak out, I stuffed it with food, mainly sweets, as if to replace the sweetness missing in my life. The image of a one-pound bar of chocolate I bought when I was twelve with money from my chores never left me, the first of many sweets that I purchased and hid over the years. I kept them in my desk, a piece of furniture that adjoined the bed where I was frequently raped.

Until I turned twelve, I had been strong and fit with a medium-sized body. Over time, I kept gaining weight, and I was miserable. No one asked me how I was doing nor checked in to see what was going on. I did not have a way to deal with the trauma I experienced. Without any examination of what was causing this change, my weight became the family issue. I was literally the elephant in the room, a room filled with slender and attractive people.

Once a year, I was lucky to have compassion modeled for me by my relatives in Israel, especially my grandparents, who we visited every summer. In contrast to my father, my grandfather, Abba, was calm, deliberate, and soft spoken. I recall playing checkers with him. Since he didn't own a checkerboard, we made one. I sat by his side on the porch as he evenly measured out the squares, and I filled in the black ones. Then, we played.

My grandmother was also very different from my mother. Her love for me was unconditional, and she accepted me for who I was, no matter how I looked and how much I weighed. When I began to gain weight, my mother was horrified and tried to restrict my diet. She hid sweets from me, an ineffective tactic leading to the chocolate bar in the desk. In contrast, when I slept over at my grandmother's house, she always left a little packet of candies wrapped in a colorful paper napkin tied with a purple bow by my bed, purple being our shared favorite color.

Unfortunately, I was with my relatives only one month out of the year. The rest of the time, school and my close relationship with my younger sister, who I loved simply without confusion or fear, were my only respite from an abusive and cold home environment.

When I was fourteen, I missed my period. Terrified, I waited several months for it to return. I absolutely knew I would kill myself if I were pregnant and had to have my brother's baby. Before the missed period, I had taken a few Tylenols in a completely half-hearted suicide attempt. Now, my desperation was much worse. A biology teacher at my high school had posted a list of community clinics that provided pregnancy tests and sexually transmitted infection (STI) testing, and I located a community health clinic on the Lower East Side of New York City. My plan was to get a pregnancy test and, if it was positive, figure out how to get an abortion. No one would know.

The clinic was an unfamiliar environment. Entering the waiting room, I was frightened and overwhelmed by the other patients, including a gay male couple loudly arguing with each other and gesticulating wildly. This was a side of New York I had never seen before. I sat in my seat, waiting to be called in to be examined, feeling very alone, yet also feeling determined to take care of things.

An old male doctor performed my first pelvic exam. It was excruciatingly painful. When I started having regular pelvic exams, I tried to understand what he had done to make it so uncomfortable. I never could. Once I became a doctor, I made sure no patient of mine would ever feel that way.

Days later, I got the results from the pregnancy test. It was negative. And, several weeks later, I finally got my period. I hid this time of extreme stress and worry from everyone, and I continued to keep silent about the abuse, which continued until my brother left for college. No one knew about my fear of pregnancy. No one knew about my trip to the clinic. And no one knew about my incredible relief when I saw blood on my underpants.

Years after the abuse ended, I finally confronted my brother. At first, he denied everything, but eventually, he admitted it and expressed remorse. However, I continued to protect my parents from the knowledge that their son was a rapist. I was in my forties when my mother asked me why I was so "mean" to my brother. That's when I finally told her. She claimed she had had no idea what had happened, that she was oblivious to the abuse in my bedroom while she was watching TV in the next room, or in the car while my father was driving. I believed her, because by then I knew how strong the power of denial can be. If you can't tolerate the thought of being pregnant, then you are not. And if you can't tolerate the thought that your son is abusing your daughter, then he is not.

By the time I was ready to tell my father, he was sick and fragile. It seemed cruel to tell him, and once again, I decided to protect others and kept silent. Given the circumstances, I think that was the right decision.

My childhood experiences laid the foundation for my career as a provider of abortion care. Since then, I've processed the trauma; I have found love and I've experienced joy. But the experiences I went through as a child brought me to where I am today and have deeply influenced my work. Sitting with patients as they told me their stories, I viscerally understood the terror of an unwanted pregnancy and the desperation that follows. I knew what it felt like to be unsupported, isolated, and to have no one to turn to. I empathized with the teenagers who hid their pregnancy from themselves and others. I identified with all the patients who were desperate. And I understood the out-of-control feeling that many of my patients had, whether they were ending the pregnancy because their baby was unhealthy or because of their difficult life circumstances. They all had a story, just like I did.

As a result, in every interaction I had with patients, I wanted them to know and feel that they were heard. I wanted them to feel that I cared *about* them as I cared *for* them. I always aspired to treat patients as I would want to be treated as a patient. But now I realize that I also aspired to treat patients as I would have wished to have been treated as an abused, frightened girl—that is, with understanding, an open heart, and compassion.

It did not take long before my experience as a teenager led me to become involved in women's health. The first step was to leave New York and my childhood trauma behind. An influential high school teacher had attended the University of Wisconsin–Madison, so I decided to apply. I was accepted and enrolled with no idea what to expect. All I knew was that Wisconsin sounded far enough away.

There, among the politically active student community, I began volunteering at the Women's Transit Authority (WTA)—a free nighttime ride service for women staffed entirely by women—and I grew increasingly interested in the newly formed women's studies program at the university. Surrounded by other politically conscious women, and, specifically, by the many lesbian feminist volunteers at the WTA, I found myself able to acknowledge my own sexuality and come out as a lesbian. I also became a volunteer at the local community health center as a patient advocate, and it was there that I was exposed to the burgeoning women's healthcare movement.

The focus of the movement was to wrest control of healthcare, particularly gynecologic care, away from the mostly male medical establishment and put it into the hands of women. Activists hoped to demystify medicine and to make it accessible and comprehensible to female patients. In communities across the country, groups of women formed collectives and opened women's clinics offering basic gynecologic care. They hosted feminist consciousness-raising groups and self-help groups, in which women gathered with plastic speculums and mirrors to look at their own and each other's cervices to better understand their bodies. Through education and consciousness raising, the goal went beyond offering direct services; the movement sought a revolutionary change in healthcare and, eventually, in our society.

I became involved with Madison's local community health center. It held a women's clinic once a week, staffed by local volunteer healthcare providers, that offered basic gynecologic care. I was a patient advocate, which meant that I accompanied each patient during their interaction with the doctor, offering support and, if needed, translating "medicalese" into standard English. In retrospect, this was comical. The doctors who volunteered at the clinic were all excellent communicators, able to explain things in a way that the patients could understand. Yet this was the dichotomy of the times. Doctors were professionals, representatives of a patriarchal system that chronically ignored women's needs. Lay health workers were nonprofessionals who helped women regain control over their bodies and care.

At the health center, I was excited by the work while appreciating that it was part of a larger mission and movement. There I learned about the Los Angeles Feminist Women's Health Center, a clinic that was at the vanguard of the women's health movement. It was founded in 1971 by Lorraine Rothman and Carol Downer, two housewives-turned-activists, who had opened their own clinic and formed the Federation of Feminist Women's Health Centers that inspired groups around the country to open clinics of their own. Together, they developed a menstrual extraction device, the Del-Em, designed for home use, that allowed women to remove their period, or even an early pregnancy, in one sitting.[1] It was easy to put together and embodied the shift that the women's health movement advocated—allowing women to control their own care and bypass clinics, doctors' offices, and hospitals. Although abortion had been legal in California since 1967, it was not widely available. The Del-Em could potentially change that by providing an option that more women could access.

Volunteering at the Madison clinic and learning about feminist clinics showed me that healthcare could be provided differently from the care I received at the Lower East Side clinic. I was drawn to the idea of combining my political ideals with practical work. I began taking science classes with the goal of eventually attending school to become a physician assistant. A physician assistant is a licensed healthcare provider, distinguished from a physician by years of education and training. I thought this credential was the perfect compromise. I would be able to provide healthcare to women without betraying my feminist principles. There was no need to become a doctor and join the male medical establishment.

CHAPTER 3

Tuesday Morning,
Maternal Indications

To my little princess,

I don't know if you are for sure a girl but since I
found out I was pregnant, I felt you were. I don't
want you thinking I didn't want you or love you. I
just knew our lives wouldn't be safe and I'd never
want anything to happen to us. I know you're in a
better place not waiting for me. In time baby girl. ♥

I love you. You'll always be in my heart.

Mom

—ANONYMOUS PATIENT

This week, in addition to the fetal-indication patients, there are also three maternal-indication patients. They are Laura, Irene, and Noor, and they are all ending their pregnancies because of severe challenges and complications they and their families face.

When I enter a room to meet maternal-indication patients, I expect them to be as tired and scared as fetal-indication patients, but I also often notice glimmers of impending relief. This pregnancy usually has not been welcome. It has been a burden the woman has been carrying, both physically and emotionally, that she desperately needs to end for her and her family's survival. For a fetal-indication patient, the pregnancy is usually known to many, but the decision to have an abortion is known by few. In contrast, for a maternal-indication patient, the pregnancy has often been hidden, and not infrequently, no one knows that she is at the clinic.

I sense only despair when I see Laura, and I'm curious to hear her story.

LAURA

Laura looks worn out and weary when I meet her, as if she's had a hard life. She is a thirty-seven-year-old white woman from East Texas and a mother of four. Her fingernails are bitten to the quick. She appears agitated. She's wearing sunglasses and a heavy long-sleeved shirt despite it being the middle of summer. She tells me a story that, unfortunately, I hear more and more frequently. It is a story of spousal abuse. And it's a story of the barriers to accessing abortion, which are different from person to person and state to state, but which often lead to abortions later in pregnancy.

For years, Laura's husband has been abusing her, both physically and emotionally. As we talk, and as Laura becomes more comfortable in this space, she rolls up her sleeves and I see multiple bruises on her arms, in varied stages of healing. Eventually, she takes off her sunglasses and reveals a cut under her left eye.

She found out she was pregnant at about eight weeks and knew right away that she had to have an abortion. Given her life circumstances, she felt that she just could not handle a fifth child but kept this belief, as well as the fact that she was pregnant, from her husband. This relationship was so abusive that Laura was literally trapped in her home with very few chances to escape, even to go to the doctor. The laws have since changed in Texas, but at that time, Laura could have accessed an abortion. She was early enough in her pregnancy to have had a medication abortion, which is a safe, two-medication regimen that induces a miscarriage.[1] Although this regimen could have been administered via telemedicine or in one clinic visit, Texas required *three* in-clinic visits and banned telemedicine for abortions. Laura couldn't justify three medical appointments to her husband.

Laura came up with a plan. She found a nearby state that required only one appointment and told her husband she would be visiting an ailing relative. When she arrived at the clinic, she learned that they only accepted cash, which she didn't have. Laura's mom, who knew of and supported her plan, had lent her a credit card—a necessity since Laura's husband controlled their bank account. But now even that plan didn't work.

By the time Laura was able to gather the cash, more time had gone by, and she was past the gestational limit for abortion in the second state. So, Laura went to another clinic in a third state. But to her surprise, that state required a twenty-four-hour waiting period between the time of signing the consent and the abortion procedure itself. She couldn't stay away from her husband that long, so she returned home.

Several weeks passed before Laura could sneak away again, but at this point, she learned that she was four days past the third state's gestational limit. Once more, she was turned away.

Before she was sent home, she was given a referral to Southwestern Women's Options, and through great effort, she managed to find her way to our clinic. Laura, like many of the patients who come to the clinic, is stressed about the cost of the abortion. A five-minute first-trimester abortion that would have cost $700 if she had been able to access it initially has become a three- to four-day third-trimester abortion, a procedure that costs at least $8,000, depending on the gestational age of the pregnancy. If a patient is from New Mexico, the New Mexico Medicaid program will cover the cost of the abortion, but with increasing restrictions, and now with abortion bans, most third-trimester patients (including Laura) come from out of state, so this coverage is not available to them.

Very few patients pay the full cost of the procedure. Many, including Laura, are able to tap into abortion funds, nonprofit organizations mostly supported by individual donations, that cover at least part of the cost. Those who don't qualify for funding yet still can't afford the abortion are offered a no-interest loan by the clinic for part of the cost and a reduced fee. But it's not just the cost of the abortion itself that needs to be addressed; there is also the lost income for missed work, plus childcare, travel, and lodging costs. Practical support groups offer assistance, but they are unable to fill in all the gaps. A third-trimester abortion is still a large financial burden for most patients. And, in Laura's case, it also comes with the risk of being caught by her abusive husband.

Laura is a ball of tension. I listen, and I reassure. She needs everything to go smoothly this week so that she can go home pretending that nothing happened. I will do everything I can to make that happen.

IRENE

I next meet Irene, a thirty-four-year-old Cuban American from Florida. In contrast to Laura, she appears almost tranquil. She is a single mother of a sixteen-year-old girl. Four years ago, Irene was treated for early-stage stomach cancer, an unusual cancer for someone her age. She'd since been in remission, but over the last few months, she'd begun to experience nausea, fatigue, and bloating. She'd also missed her periods, though since completing her cancer treatment, it was normal for her to have only several periods a year. At first, she thought the fatigue and other symptoms were simply the result of her stressful life. The cancer was now at bay, but life was still hard. Now, in addition to caring for her daughter, to whom she is deeply attached, Irene works two minimum-wage jobs and is going to school part time with the goal of becoming a nurse anesthetist. Irene's financial situation is precarious, but she and her daughter make do, and Irene is intent on helping her daughter go to college.

When Irene's symptoms, especially the bloating, persisted and worsened, she feared that the cancer may have recurred. And, in fact, it had. She was scheduled for a new round of chemotherapy. But the pre-chemotherapy lab work also showed something else: she was pregnant.

Irene told me that she was shocked, yet in retrospect, it all made sense to her. The symptoms of the cancer recurrence were also pregnancy symptoms! But the possibility of pregnancy was the furthest thing from her mind. Caring for her daughter and her own health were at the forefront. It never occurred to her to take a pregnancy test.

Irene's doctor told her that she should start chemotherapy as soon as possible, but she could not start it while pregnant. Her choices were stark: continue the pregnancy to term, allowing the cancer to progress and risk her life, or end the pregnancy as soon as possible and start chemotherapy. For Irene, the decision was clear. Her daughter still needed her. Irene would do anything necessary to prolong her life and continue to mother her child. Unfortunately, by the time the pregnancy was diagnosed, she was early in the third trimester, just past Florida's gestational limit at the time. The local abortion clinic that was forced to turn her down referred her to our clinic.

I listen to her heartbreaking story, which she relates in a matter-of-fact manner. She is calm, but I inwardly seethe, angry that she could not be cared for in her home state of Florida and has had to travel to Albuquerque for this necessary care. Nevertheless, I maintain a game face. I answer her questions and sign the consents. I leave and ask the counselor to prepare her for the exam. That leaves just one last patient to see this morning.

NOOR

I walk into the room and see a sullen-looking young woman who tosses her long, dark hair back repeatedly while we talk. Noor is a seventeen-year-old college student from Ohio. She is a first-generation American whose parents emigrated from Iran. Unbeknownst to her parents, she has had a steady boyfriend for the past two years. They were using condoms for birth control and used Plan B, the emergency contraception, the one time they didn't use a condom. Plan B can lower the risk of pregnancy by up to 87 percent, which is good but is still not 100 percent. When her period didn't come, Noor took a pregnancy test, which was positive.

Noor comes from a very traditional family, and because her parents expected her to remain a virgin until marriage, she didn't think she could tell them she was pregnant. But she also felt strongly that continuing the pregnancy was not an option and tried to figure out how to access an abortion. She assumed she would be disowned by her family and ostracized by her community. And while she liked her boyfriend, she did not feel ready to have a child or to be a parent with him.

Although Noor was in college, she lived at home under her parents' unceasing scrutiny. Her state required minors to obtain the consent of at least one parent before having an abortion. However, she didn't believe she could talk to her parents. Instead, she tried to get a judicial bypass, which involves going in front of a judge and asking for permission to obtain an abortion without parental involvement. Noor missed several appointments with the judge because she couldn't sneak out of her house. Eventually she did, and the judge affirmed her decision to have an abortion, granting her waiver request.

When she finally made it to a clinic, she was too far along. She was no longer eligible for a medication abortion, and despite help from her boyfriend, she couldn't raise the additional money for an in-clinic abortion, so she gave up. Noor hid the pregnancy from her family by wearing sweatpants and hoodies. It was her first semester at college, and rather than enjoy the new world she had entered, she retreated into herself so that no one would suspect.

"What did you think would happen once you started going into labor?" I ask Noor gently. She stares at me blankly. "I don't know. I hadn't thought that far." This answer does not surprise me; it's what most teenagers in her position tell me. Noor was just living day by day, expending all her energy hiding the pregnancy. The future was unfathomable.

But Noor's mother eventually grew suspicious and one day confronted her daughter, holding up several clean tampons she had fished from the trash. (Until I started working in abortion care, I never realized how many mothers check the tampons and menstrual pads in the bathroom garbage can.) Her mother brought home a pregnancy test for Noor and pressured her to take it in front of her. Of course, it was positive. As Noor expected, her mother was disappointed and angry, but Noor did *not* expect that both her parents would support her decision to have an abortion. Her mother went with her to a local clinic, which referred Noor to a clinic in a different state, but she was too far along for that state too.

Finally, Noor was referred to Southwestern Women's Options. She sits in front of me, next to her father, Kareem. They are sitting at opposite ends of the couch, separated by a stony silence. They barely look at each other. I hope that at some point during their time in Albuquerque they will start warming up to one another.

As I typically do when I care for a teenager, I first meet Noor with her accompanying parent. Usually, that parent is a mother; less commonly, both parents; or, rarely, only a father. Kareem explains that Noor's mother could not get leave from work. Even though the girl is my patient, I believe it's important that parents have an opportunity to meet the doctor taking care of their daughter. Then, after I've answered their questions, I always ask the parents to leave the room.

Noor is slightly anemic, so I explain to her and Kareem that her blood count is a little low. "This does not mean that you will bleed more heavily during the abortion than someone who has a normal blood count," I explain. "It *does* mean, though, that if you do bleed heavily, you are at higher risk for needing a blood transfusion than someone who is not anemic. Think of it as if your gas tank isn't completely full." I go on to explain that if Noor did need a blood transfusion, we would transfer her to the hospital five minutes away. Though extremely unlikely, mild anemia puts her at a slightly higher risk of needing a transfusion or hysterectomy and of death. But all of that is extremely rare, I reassure them. "Talking about it does not mean that it will happen."

Noor looks scared. Kareem looks stoic. I repeat that the risks of these major complications are rare. Then I have Kareem step out of the room. I always make sure to speak privately with a patient like Noor to find out whether there is anything she wants to tell or ask me that she hasn't felt comfortable saying in front of her parents. I let her know that, although I might also speak to her parent privately, I will not share anything that she discloses. Most importantly, I want to ensure that she has decided to have an abortion of her own volition, that no one is coercing her.

Once her father leaves, Noor visibly relaxes and opens up about her life. She tells me how grateful she is to finally be able to end this pregnancy. Until her parents found out, her boyfriend was the only person who knew she was pregnant, and it was getting harder and harder to hide it at home and at college. She tells me she could feel her mental state slipping. She stopped eating, slept poorly, and rarely showered. She spent innumerable hours ruminating about this unwanted pregnancy, and it was a relief when her parents found out that she was pregnant. The hiding was now over. It was an even bigger relief when they supported her decision to have an abortion.

I was in my twenties when I was first introduced to abortion care as a counselor at an abortion clinic. At that time, I related to patients as a peer. As the years went by, as I became a doctor and I aged, my relationship to patients, and their relationship to me, changed. Mainly it was because I had become the professional responsible for their well-being. But at times I also felt a different connection, which I feel with Noor, a mother-daughter dynamic (or, by the time I retired, *grandmother*-daughter). I sense that she relates to me as the idealized "good mother," the one who doesn't judge and is all-accepting, as opposed to her real mother, with whom she has a complicated relationship.

After we talk, Noor does not have anything else to ask outside of her father's presence. She is adamant that this is her decision and that no one is coercing her. She feels ready to proceed with the abortion.

CHAPTER 4

California: 1970s–2000s

Abortion is not a cerebral or a reproductive
issue. Abortion is a matter of the heart.

—GEORGE R. TILLER, MD

I arrived in Los Angeles to start a summer internship at the LA
Feminist Women's Health Center on June 17, 1979. I was a twenty-
two-year-old idealist just where I wanted to be—at the epicenter
of feminist healthcare—and I was eager to learn all that I could
that summer.

At the clinic, the environment was vibrant and collaborative.
The center's goal was to break down barriers between patients and
healthcare providers, delivering care from woman to woman—
among equals. To that end, all services, aside from abortion care,
were provided by health workers in a group setting, be they annual pap and pelvic exams, checks for vaginal infections, or birth
control counseling. The group sessions weren't just designed to
provide care but also to educate women about their bodies. During
my first shift, at the end of the visit, a health worker took out a
plastic speculum, a hand mirror, and a flashlight. She inserted the
speculum and, to the group, described her hidden anatomy. "The
round ball is the cervix, the bottom part of the uterus. The small
opening is called the os. That's where menstrual blood comes out
of if you have a period and what opens wide enough to let a baby
pass though if you deliver."

This was part of the clinic's routine, and each time, I saw women
in the group light up with amazement and awe. This was a part of

their body that had been hidden, unknown, and often shrouded in shame. No one had taken the time to explain it before.

Only when I received a copy of the weekly schedule did I realize that, although it offered routine gynecologic care, the clinic's main focus was abortions. The clinic performed first-trimester abortions and was about to expand its services to provide second-trimester abortions. I was taken aback; I wasn't expecting that. But then I was interested; here was something new I could learn.

At the LA Feminist Women's Health Center, abortion care began with a pregnancy test done in a group setting. The health worker introduced herself to the group of three to four women— and those seeking care were called *women*, not *patients*, in contrast to the terminology used in other clinical settings. She explained that she was not a doctor and that there was nothing mysterious about performing a pregnancy test, even though at the time they were only available through medical facilities. The women then ran their own tests. After determining the results, the group had a discussion about their options, including abortion.

The groups were often intense and eye-opening. In the first group I observed, Maeve, an Irish woman visiting California, burst into what I initially thought was laughter when she saw her positive results. But she wasn't laughing. She was sobbing. In Ireland, abortion was illegal. (It was only legalized there in 2018.) Women were forced to travel to England for abortions, and Maeve thought she would have to do that, even though she lacked the financial resources. She was tremendously relieved when the group told her that abortion was legal in the United States and that the price was reasonable.

Before observing and participating in the sessions, I felt dubious that a group setting was appropriate for such a private and often emotional moment. However, I came to see its benefits. It allowed women in the group to share their experiences in a supportive environment and to learn from one another. I also realized, however, that one woman's anxieties could heighten the fears of others. It took a skilled facilitator to provide accurate information and reassurance, which were the ultimate goals of the group sessions.

The abortion clinic I observed in the first week of my internship was life-changing for me. Perhaps it seems surprising that a lesbian would be interested in abortion care. After all, the women we cared for were overwhelmingly heterosexual. Yet most of the staff at the clinic were lesbians, and they were all feminists. To me, the connection was clear. Whether the question was to continue or end a pregnancy, or to have sex with men or with women, the issue at stake was autonomy. We sought the ability to take control of our lives and our bodies, regardless of societal norms and expectations.

At the clinic, every part of the process, except for the abortion itself, was managed by the health workers. All women scheduled for an abortion that day sat together in an open room where a health worker explained the procedure.[1] When the women were brought, one by one, to the procedure room, there were always two health workers in the room. One was assigned to the woman, to hold her hand, comfort her, and guide her through the process. The second health worker's job was to assist the doctor, handing them instruments, and, once the abortion was completed, to bring the pregnancy tissue to a health worker in the lab where it was examined.

Health workers rotated through all the jobs during the abortion clinic. My favorite role, I soon realized, was to support women during the procedure. To be with someone at a vulnerable time, to offer comfort and to witness a transformative moment in a woman's life, was both intimate and intense. I had found my life's calling.

While assisting during the abortion procedures at the clinic, I observed the physicians who worked there and considered their role. They were all male, with one exception. On the whole, they were viewed as mere technicians, whose only job was to sit down at the foot of the table, keep quiet, empty the uterus, and leave the rest to the female health workers. Yet without the physicians, there would be no abortion clinic. This awareness took time to percolate, but it had a big effect on me.

Over the course of the summer, I learned that the LA Feminist Women's Health Center was gearing up to start offering second-trimester abortions. The clinic already conducted abortions in the first trimester, up to twelve to fourteen weeks, by suction aspiration. But if a woman missed that window, she would have to wait until the sixteenth week of pregnancy for a saline abortion, a lengthy process often taking more than twenty-four hours, with a high risk of complications. A newer method, dilation and evacuation (D&E), was performed using instruments to remove the pregnancy, offering a safer and quicker procedure that could take minutes rather than hours. This was the method the clinic was hoping to introduce, and I became interested in the technical aspects of the D&E procedure.

Given the clinic's attitude toward doctors, who were viewed as hired hands, it was ironic that the longer I worked there, the more interested I grew in becoming one. It seemed to be the missing piece of the women's healthcare movement I'd joined. I wanted to continue to provide the emotional care and support patients needed. But I also wanted to be able to perform the actual procedure. My experience at the clinic and as a teenager in New York underscored the difference that a supportive environment could make. What if I could become an abortion provider who understood the full picture? I was grateful for my experience at the LA Feminist Women's Health Center, but by the end of the summer, it was time to move on.

Back in Madison, I changed my plans. Instead of finishing up my prerequisites and applying to physician assistant programs, I applied to medical schools.

I ended up accepting a position at a medical school in Israel, where I lived on the same block as the hospital where I was born and five minutes away from my beloved grandmother. After graduating, I returned to Madison in 1986 for a three-year residency training in family medicine.

Based on my experiences in medical school, I was looking forward to my rotation in obstetrics. But I did not realize how powerfully it would affect me or how conflicted my feelings would be.

From my first day of the rotation, I was drawn to the beauty of birth. Caring for the women on the obstetrics ward, I experienced the same sense of intimacy and intensity that I'd felt as a health worker at the LA Feminist Women's Health Center while supporting women during their abortions. It was awe inspiring, but my respect and admiration for the laboring woman was tempered by another feeling. The mothers in the hospital were often confined to a bed, tangled in monitoring equipment and unable to move. Throughout the labor, the doctor, rather than the birthing woman, was in control of the delivery. Even in these moments of beauty, she seemed to me to be subjugated.

I wanted to know whether there was an alternative. As long as things were going well, I wondered, why couldn't the natural process of birth unfold without constant interference and intervention? And if women could deliver without unnecessary medical intervention, what would that be like?

As the year went on, I realized that I wouldn't be able to answer this question in a hospital setting. If I wanted to witness a different model for birth—one where the mother, rather than the doctor, could lead—I would need another change of course. After my intern year, I made an unusual decision: I would take a year off from residency to explore home birth and midwifery.

In February 1987, I left the freezing cold of Madison and landed in beautiful, sunny San Francisco. I rented a car to drive seventy miles along the coast to Santa Cruz, where Kate Bowland, a nurse midwife, had agreed to take me on as her apprentice. I arrived in Santa Cruz with many preconceptions about what home birth would entail, including candlelit birthing rooms and placenta-eating rituals. I also had assumptions about what a home birth midwife would be like. I imagined an ethereal, wispy white woman with long flowing hair who spoke and trod softly. Kate did not fit my stereotype at all. She was big, loud, and bossy, as well as blunt, funny, and to the point.

Kate and I hit it off immediately. In our time together, I learned so much more than what I had been taught in medical school and residency about pregnancy and birth. Kate and I developed close relationships with each of our clients and their families. Prenatal visits lasted a minimum of thirty minutes, and we used that time to get to know the woman and her family before the birth. If the woman had given birth before, we learned about those births as well. I found out what was most important to her, what she was most afraid of, and what past traumas I should be aware of. By recognizing these before the birth, we could address them if they arose at the birth itself.

Our clients grew comfortable in the knowledge that we, who they had come to know and trust, would be there to attend the birth. This scenario was very different from standard obstetric practices, in which prenatal visits are often five minutes long and, depending on the call schedule, there is no guarantee that the birthing woman and the physician who attends her birth will have ever met previously.

Working for Kate, I learned about the mechanics of birth, and I learned about the strong emotions of birth. Most of all, I learned patience—patience during the laboring process and patience for *my* learning process. In birth, things happen at their own pace and on their own terms, which can often be unpredictable.

Early in my time in Santa Cruz, Kate and I cared for a woman who lived far up in the Santa Cruz mountains in a home without running water or electricity. Because of the remoteness, the plan was for her to deliver at Kate's homey clinic in town. One day, she called Kate to say that her contractions had begun, and Kate told her to come into town. Her partner put her into their van and began a mad dash to the clinic. I was to meet them there.

I arrived just as the van pulled up. The woman was already in strong labor, and her partner was frantic. Kate was not yet there to help. Despite my rotation in obstetrics, I had no idea what to do. Should I help her deliver in the van? Should I get her out of the van? But I didn't have keys to the clinic. So what should I do?

I could only manage to hover around until Kate arrived and took charge. She got into the van, helped the woman into the clinic, and went on to deliver a healthy baby. Afterward, I felt foolish. How could I have been so flustered? Wouldn't everyone respond as Kate did, so effortlessly, so naturally? Over time I learned that things only appear to come expertly through study and repetition. It was experience that allowed practitioners like Kate to act calmly and deliberately. This is what I aspired to.

Instead of working with Kate for a year, as I originally anticipated, I ended up spending two years in Santa Cruz. In addition to working with Kate, I attended births with several other midwives, allowing me to see different approaches to midwifery and the birthing process.

It was through Kate that I met Julie, my future wife. Originally from Kansas, Julie had practiced midwifery for years in a nearby farmworker community and was working there as a physician assistant in a clinic. Julie didn't fit my midwife stereotype either. Her long, curly black hair puffed outward. Her brown eyes were soulful and penetrating. In typical lesbian fashion at the time, we met for tea on our first unofficial date. She was smart, kind, and intense. I was very attracted to the first two characteristics and, initially, scared by the third. Thirty-five years later, Julie's hair is white, but everything else I initially admired about her has remained and grown. And her intensity is now something that I greatly appreciate.

The two years I spent as a midwife in Santa Cruz fundamentally shaped my approach to healthcare. This period built on the foundation laid in LA and informed my later approach to third-trimester abortion care. Both experiences taught me the importance of treating patients with respect and speaking to them in everyday language. More importantly, both the healthcare workers in LA and the midwives in Santa Cruz strove to empower women in potentially vulnerable situations, be that a gyn exam, an abortion, or a birth. As the survivor of childhood abuse who for years felt that I had no control over my body, I resonated deeply with this objective.

The midwifery model, which can be applied to both birth and abortion, is centered on honoring and supporting the woman as she goes through the experience. By working with midwives, I learned that the attendant's role is to maintain a calm and reassuring presence and to decrease stimuli to allow the process to unfold. The woman's active participation in her own process is paramount. And the patient's well-being is more than physical; it is emotional and spiritual as well. All these dimensions are part of good care, and for the rest of my career, I sought to incorporate all three.

By 1989, I was ready to return to medicine. I felt that I understood how to attend to a woman giving birth when all was going well, but I also wanted to learn how to handle the complications, which could make a lifesaving difference. Instead of going back to my family medicine residency in Wisconsin, I made the decision to become an obstetrician-gynecologist and to do so in California to be closer to Julie. I left Santa Cruz and headed to Oakland to begin an OB-GYN residency.

Residency was a jarring contrast to attending home births. It was exhausting and soul sucking. As residents, we were on call every third or fourth night, which meant working thirty-six hours at a time. Grueling as this schedule was, I knew it was something I had to get through. Mainly what I remember of those four years is how Julie cared for me and carried me through that time. After two months, she moved to Oakland and worked as a midwife at Oakland's public hospital. When she wasn't working and I was on call, she brought me coffee and espresso brownies to keep me going. When I got home, barely awake, she fed me soup and put me to bed.

One of my hopes during residency was that I would finally learn how to perform abortions. It was now ten years after my summer at the LA Feminist Women's Health Center, the summer that opened my eyes to abortion care. My subsequent interest in midwifery hadn't deterred me from the path toward becoming an abortion provider. These two passions, birth and abortion, were both rooted in my fervent belief that women should be able to decide if they want to be pregnant and give birth or not—and, if they do, how. Even so, I couldn't yet imagine that as a provider of third-trimester abortions, I would eventually be able to synthesize elements of these two seemingly disparate aspects of care.

At the time, learning how to perform abortions was not a requirement for OB-GYN residency programs. Indeed, when I was a resident, such training was haphazard and often difficult to find. I tried to be involved with as many abortion cases as possible and to take on any abortion patients who were transferred to the hospital from clinics.

I performed my first abortion in 1990 as a second-year resident. The patient was in her twenties, and it was her first pregnancy. In contrast to the outpatient abortions at the LA Feminist Women's Health Center, this abortion was performed in the hospital's operating room, and the patient was put to sleep. When I did the pelvic exam, I could feel that the patient's uterus was tilted backward, a completely normal but less common position and one that can make it technically more challenging to remove a pregnancy. Realizing this, I asked the supervising attending physician to be in the room with me. As he stood by me, a dilator I was using to open the patient's cervix went through the wall of her uterus, causing a perforation. Thankfully, it was a benign perforation that didn't require any treatment beyond observation, but I still felt terrible. I spent years studying to become a doctor in order to provide abortion care—and the first thing I did was cause a complication.

As I walked out of the operating room, I was full of doubt. *Was I meant to do this work? Was this a sign?* Upon further reflection, I realized this likely wasn't a sign that I should stop, but rather it was a sign that I needed to improve my technique. After I took a step back, I redoubled my efforts. By seeking out all the cases I could, I managed to receive enough training in abortion care to feel fairly confident in my skills. But I knew I needed more direct training. I started to keep an eye out for a mentor.

In my last year of residency, I met Dr. Jim McMahon, the owner of Eve Surgical Center, a clinic offering all-trimester abortion care in Los Angeles. At the Eve clinic, women were treated like people, not like objects waiting with their legs open for someone to remove an unwanted pregnancy. I called to set up a visit and was invited to stay for a week of observation. That week opened up a whole new world for me.

The clinic was set up thoughtfully. To represent that the paths we take in life are not always linear, the walkway to the front door was curved rather than straight. In the private waiting area, there was a continuously running slideshow of the four seasons, designed to remind patients that, although in the moment things might be bleak, winter is always followed by spring and summer. Time passes, life moves on, and we heal. The warm and comforting atmosphere inside the clinic was completely different from the cold, sterile atmosphere of a hospital.

Dr. McMahon routinely performed abortions for fetal anomalies at advanced gestational ages and sought to do so in the most compassionate way possible. Seeking to offer women the chance to hold the fetus and grieve their loss, he developed an abortion procedure called intact dilation and extraction (D&X), in which the fetus was removed as a whole rather than being removed in several pieces, as in traditional dilation and evacuation (D&E).[2] These procedures also made it possible to perform a careful autopsy after the abortion and get a precise diagnosis of any fetal anomalies, which could be very helpful information for the woman and her doctor.

Over the course of the week, Dr. McMahon introduced me to this procedure. He exposed me to a new approach to abortion care later in pregnancy, but he also showed me a different *kind* of abortion care. Dr. McMahon maintained a laser-like focus on the woman rather than on the demands of the institution, and in doing so, he prioritized the woman's emotional, spiritual, and physical well-being. I had missed that level of care since leaving midwifery in Santa Cruz. Dr. McMahon's approach to abortion care was exactly what I had been looking for.

The week I spent with Dr. McMahon came late in my residency. By then, I had already lined up a job to become an ob-gyn in the Bay Area. But I knew that I wanted to work with him at Eve Surgical Center, and I promised to stay in touch.

A few months later, in June 1993, I completed residency. It was a time for celebration after four very long years. Less than a week later, Julie and I got married at a friend's house by the water. Same-sex marriage was not legal at the time, so we billed it as a matrimony instead. It was a Jewish ceremony, complete with Hebrew prayers and huppah.

Following our wedding, I began working as an ob-gyn, providing full-scope care at both a community clinic and a hospital. However, I soon found myself unhappy with the work. In the clinic, I was spending most of my time having discussions about the pros and cons of hormone replacement therapy for menopausal women. Meanwhile, at the hospital, obstetrics seemed harried and brusque in comparison to the births I'd seen as a midwife. And the question was never how to avoid unnecessary cesarean sections but rather when to proceed with them.

I still hoped to return to Eve Surgical Center with Dr. McMahon, and throughout my first year of practice, he and I discussed the possibility of me joining his practice. But tragically, he was diagnosed with an aggressive cancer and succumbed to it in 1995. I mourned, and I let my dream go. Instead, I spent seven years as an unfulfilled ob-gyn. Although I loved caring for patients, the chasm between my beliefs and my practice only widened as time went by.

One day, while walking by my favorite pastry shop in the East Bay, I noticed a help-wanted ad in the window and applied for the job. Although acknowledging that I was overqualified, the owner graciously offered me part-time work between shifts at the hospital, and for a while it helped. The shop, with its beautiful cakes and its soft music, was a welcome refuge from the sterile environment, bright lights, and endless overhead pages of the hospital.

Eventually, however, the relief of the pastry shop wasn't enough. I realized that I needed to be engaged in work I felt passionately about. So in 2000, in my early forties, I left my general OB-GYN practice to embark on a second career, returning to what drew me to medicine in the first place: abortion care.

CHAPTER 5

Tuesday Afternoon

I've heard thousands and thousands and tens of
thousands of women share their desperation, their
anxiety, their tension, their feeling that their life as they
know it is going to be expended, is going to evaporate
and vanish in front of their eyes. I've never heard a fetus
talk to me. You know who's talking to me? It is the
patient and, in my book, the woman is the patient.

—GEORGE R. TILLER, MD

Group sessions were an important part of the care I observed at the LA Feminist Women's Health Center and, later, during my time with Dr. Tiller. I saw how powerful and reassuring group sessions were for patients and their support people. The sessions offered patients the opportunity to meet others who were going through similar situations and to realize that they were not alone. Over the years, I saw how the experiences, wisdom, and care that participants shared in the groups could turn out to be profoundly helpful to others.

When I was given the opportunity to create a third-trimester abortion practice in Albuquerque, I knew group sessions would be an integral part of that care. We scheduled them each week on Tuesday afternoons, the first day of care, after I had met with each patient individually and begun the abortion process.

After leaving the clinic Tuesday morning, the third-trimester patients return to their hotels for a few hours of rest. Many of them are staying in the same hotel, but they have not yet been introduced to each other. In the afternoon, the patients return for ultrasounds to confirm that the injection has worked, after which there are counseling sessions for the two groups of patients—fetal indications and maternal indications. Each session is divided into two parts. The first part is facilitated by either me or a counselor, with the purpose of conveying information and answering questions. During the second part, the facilitator steps back, and the patients take the lead.

MATERNAL-INDICATION GROUP

Skye, one of the clinic's senior counselors, leads the group session for this week's maternal-indication patients: Irene, Laura, and Noor. She is a licensed midwife who has trained all the counselors in "gurney," the laboring room where the inductions take place. She has been instrumental in integrating the midwifery model of care into the practice, a model recognizing that a constant and reassuring presence in labor helps to reduce anxiety and improves outcomes. Skye is warm and intelligent. She conveys both compassion and competence, helping our patients know that they are in good hands.

At the start of the session, Skye greets the patients and answers questions. She explains that third-trimester abortion involves labor and delivery—in this case, of a stillborn. She reviews the process of delivery and the one-on-one labor support they will receive from a counselor who has been trained as a doula. (A doula is a person trained to provide physical and emotional support in childbirth. Abortion doulas provide that type of support for those undergoing abortions.) Skye reviews coping techniques for labor, including breathing techniques, movement, sitting or bouncing on a birthing ball, and back massage. In contrast to a standard hospital delivery, there will be no constant interruptions as different medical personnel come in and out of the room. There will be no fetal monitoring as demise has already occurred. The lights will be dimmed; the doula will speak softly. All efforts will be made to maintain a calm and peaceful atmosphere.

After explaining the process to come, Skye facilitates a conversation among the three women. For many participants in these groups, it is the first time they have been able to talk about their experiences with their peers. It is a time for unburdening, sharing, and support.

This week, I wonder how they will interact with and relate to one another. The three of them have such different life experiences and reasons for coming to the clinic. But, as Skye reports back to me later, the meeting turned out to be a round-robin of support for one another.

Laura walked into the room with her sunglasses on, just as she had for her initial meeting with me. But once she started talking to Irene and Noor about the years of abuse, she took them off. She told the group that she couldn't take the abuse any longer: "I look in the mirror and I feel bad." And yet, with her four kids and no money, she felt stuck. Irene turned to her and told her how very sorry she was for all that she had suffered, and Laura thanked her.

Then, Irene talked about her cancer diagnosis, her love for her daughter, and her fear that she would not live to see her go to college. Noor, just a year older than Irene's daughter, told her: "It will be okay. Your daughter is lucky to have you as a mother." Irene, perhaps thinking of her daughter at home, smiled.

Noor talked about the familial pressures on her to remain celibate and how difficult things were once she realized she was pregnant. She talked about how she felt the need to hide her pregnancy from her parents and her unsuccessful attempts to get an abortion on her own. She was scared and stressed for months, falling into depression.

Laura, who deeply understood those feelings, took her hand and held it. Finally, speaking to both of them and perhaps to herself, she talked about the importance of taking care of oneself. Laura said, "God understands what you're going through, and things will get better."

Skye tells me how moved she was to see how the three women cared for each other. They wanted to continue their conversation

even once the meeting ended, and they decided to have dinner together after they left the clinic. Listening to Skye, I thought—and
not for the first time—that but for the unfortunate turn of events,
these three women would never have had the opportunity to talk
to each other, let alone to comfort each other.

FETAL-INDICATION GROUP

Meanwhile, I lead the fetal-indication group. All the couples are
brought to the recovery room. No one makes eye contact at first.

I'm familiar with the heaviness that surrounds my patients at
the beginning of these group counseling sessions. I take a deep
breath and look around the room.

"All of you are here because your baby is sick," I begin. Mary
starts tearing up. "If your baby was healthy, you wouldn't be here.
Even if you don't say anything during this meeting, it helps to sit
with others who are going through the same thing as you, who
know exactly how you are feeling."

I start by telling them what to expect on the day of induction.
"Just like today, we'll give you medication through the IV for pain
and anxiety. We'll take out the dilators and check your cervix. If the
cervix is not ready, we'll place new ones and start the induction the
following day. If your cervix is ready, we'll break the bag of water
and give you a medication called misoprostol that induces labor.

"The cervix—the bottom part of the uterus—needs to shorten,
soften, and open, which is what misoprostol does. Amrita and Jamie, you've had a baby before, so you know that at term, the cervix
needs to open to ten centimeters for the baby to deliver. Right now,
in this situation, far from term, the baby is much smaller and there
is no magic number. The cervix needs to open enough for the baby
to come through."

I go on to explain that we will give them the misoprostol every
two hours and that they will gradually start to feel contractions. "The
challenge in this practice is to convince your body to go into labor.
We're telling your body that it needs to release the pregnancy before

it's biologically designed to. Sometimes, even though your cervix is ready, your body is not. And despite the medications, you don't go into labor. If there's not much change by the end of the day, we'll send you back to your hotel and restart the induction the next day."

I see some worried glances. "There is nothing wrong if that happens," I reassure them. "Usually, the next day, things go quickly. You'll have a counselor, trained in labor support techniques—a doula—with you at all times. She'll encourage you to try different positions, to move around, to walk. At some point, you'll start feeling pressure and you'll push the baby out. Unless you've told us that you want to see the baby right away—and most people want to wait until the next day—we keep you covered so that you don't see the baby as you deliver.

"After delivery—and this is different from a full-term delivery—we will bring you to one of the rooms you were in yesterday to place the dilators, and we will do a gentle dilation and curettage, a D&C. We want to empty the uterus of any fluid and want to be sure that you are not bleeding too much. Bleeding is a normal part of delivery, and we want to make sure that the amount is normal. Then, we'll bring you to the recovery room to rest for at least two hours. If everything's okay, you'll go back to your hotel and return the next day for what we call a checkout exam and to view the baby, if that's what you've chosen."

I warn them not to skip the checkout exam. "None of you are from Albuquerque, and we want to be sure that you are safe to travel home before you leave." In addition to assessing my patients physically and emotionally, the checkout exam is also time for the patient to process the week with me.

Then I broach a very important topic. Probably not many people in these patients' lives know their baby is sick and that they're about to have an abortion. Usually, only their parents and a few select friends know. Sometimes, only one set of parents is told. Sometimes, no one knows.

"I want to talk about what to tell people at home who know you are pregnant but don't know you are here. The most important thing is to take care of yourselves. This is a time to heal from this trauma. It's not a time to have discussions or arguments about abortion. You've already told the people who you know will support you. Those are the people who are in your bubble of support. You don't owe an explanation to anyone else. Whatever you decide to say, and I have some suggestions, my advice is to keep it short and simple and to be prepared with your sentences. If you are not prepared, you might end up losing it at the checkout counter of the supermarket where you've shopped for years, when the friendly cashier asks you about your baby."

Here are the four sentences I offer my patients:

The baby was sick.

We went for testing.

The baby didn't make it.

It's hard for me to talk about it right now.

I expand on my offerings. "Let's break it down. *The baby was sick.* Yes, if the baby wasn't sick, you wouldn't be here.

"*We went for testing.* Yes, that explains why you aren't home.

"*The baby didn't make it.* Yes.

"*It's hard for me to talk about it right now.* That ends the conversation. It's the period at the end of the sentence. Most of the time, when you say that, the person will say, 'I'm so sorry. Let me know if there's anything I can do.' Every once in a while, someone may want more information. Where did you go? What hospital did you go to? What was it like? The answer is, 'It's hard for me to talk about it right now.' And sometimes, you just have to walk away."

I've heard from many people over the years that they have found this advice very useful. I go on to suggest relaying the script to one person in their circle of family or friends and having that person share it with everyone else, so my patients don't have to keep having awkward and painful conversations with everyone they know.

Here, I pause for a discussion. Jamie and Robert tell the group that this is not an issue for them. Their community and both sides of their family know why they're in Albuquerque. Amrita and Arun have also been open with their decision. In contrast, Mary and Christopher have told no one. They think this script will be useful.

I proceed. "I want to talk about baby plans, what we can do after the delivery to help with the healing process. But there is no right way. There is no specific path that you must follow to be able to heal. Whatever you decide is the right way. I just ask that you carefully think about it. We have a list of things we can offer, but if there's anything else you think is important, let us know.

"For example," I tell them, "once a woman brought a talisman to put on her baby's chest. Another time a couple brought their three-year-old, and together they dressed the baby in clothes that they had brought.

"We can take footprints and handprints," I explain. "When you give birth at term, you receive a birth certificate. Here we provide a certificate of miscarriage, inscribed by one of our nurses who is skilled in calligraphy.

"We always take two sets of photos: medical photos, which focus on the baby's anomalies for your doctor or genetic counselor; and commemorative photos, which focus on the beauty of your baby. We always take them. If you don't want them, we keep them in your chart, so you can call us if you change your mind and we will send them to you. We can also say a blessing, which is spiritual, not religious, and either say it with you or give it to you. We place it—along with a candle, a receiving blanket, and a teddy bear—in a handmade pouch."

In the past, we put all of these items in a large manila envelope. But then one day, a former patient sent us a box she had decorated in which to place the memorabilia. She had made one for herself and wanted to pass this one on to our next patient. From then on, we started placing the memorabilia in a plain white box from Michaels, the hobby store. When the supply of boxes ran out during Covid, a team of volunteers started sewing pouches with beautiful fabric.

"You can change your mind about photos," I say. "But what you can't change your mind about is viewing the baby. Once you leave, you won't have another opportunity. People have different thoughts about viewing. Some don't want to see the baby. They want to hold on to the image that they have of the baby, either from ultrasounds or in their minds. For others, seeing the baby is important. If the defects are external, it can seem hard, but it can also be confirming. You will look and think to yourselves: 'This is why we came to Albuquerque.'

"If the anomalies are all internal—for example, a heart defect— the baby will look normal, although premature. That may make it easier to see the baby, but then you have to believe all the tests that were done that confirmed the diagnosis before you came here."

I explain that we usually do the viewing the day after delivery, so that patients have time to rest and recover beforehand. "We bring you and your partner to one of the counseling rooms. We describe the baby to you and tell you the anomalies we noticed, if there are any. When you are ready, we bring the baby to you. The baby will be in a basket, covered in a blanket. We put the basket in a chair facing you. When you are ready, you can lift the blanket off. What you will see is the baby's face and hands out of the blanket that is covering the baby. The rest is up to you. We ask you if you want some privacy—most people do—and we step out of the room. Everyone spends their time with the baby in a different way."

I offer the group examples of what I've seen before. "One person gazed intently at her baby for a few seconds and then said, 'I'm done.' And she was. Another took off the second blanket, counted its fingers and toes, picked up the baby, held the baby, and spent hours examining every inch of its body. When you are done, we take the baby away, and, if you would like, you can arrange for burial or cremation."

I explain that there is a local funeral home that is sympathetic to our patients. Most often, patients request cremation, but at times, they prefer a burial. It can be done locally, or the body can be shipped to a receiving funeral home in their hometown. I hand them a paper copy of the baby plan and ask them to fill it out in the hotel and return it the next day.

Then it is time to share. I go around the room, asking the participants to tell their stories. I learned early on to first pick the couple who appear most eager to talk. Once they begin, others who initially appear reticent to share their stories feel the commonality of their experiences and feel more comfortable opening their hearts. This is when the most powerful times of sharing unfold.

Today, my social icebreakers are Jamie and Robert. They tell the group what it was like learning about their baby's dismal prognosis. Soon Robert is bawling. Jamie explains how supportive their pastor and religious community have been. I glance over at Mary and Christopher, and I see Christopher nodding in agreement while Jamie talks about her faith. Mary hands Robert a box of tissues. The tissue box gets passed around a lot during this session.

Then Mary and Christopher share. They say they wish they had the same kind of support from their religious community as Jamie and Robert. They feel very alone. Christopher shares that he had been worried that the digoxin injection would hurt their baby. He feels better now that that part is over, but he still has lingering concerns about fetal pain. Amrita says that she, too, has been worried about it. The others nod in agreement. It seems that this topic needs to be addressed and I dive in.

They are not the first patients to raise this issue. I noticed that this issue started to come up for patients in all trimesters around 2010. Prior to this, patients had never raised the issue of fetal pain. But now, even at six weeks, patients sometimes ask. At first, I did not understand why, but it proved to be an issue manufactured by the anti-abortion movement, in hopes of generating public concern and more restrictive legislation. In response to their campaign, legislators in dozens of states started banning abortions after twenty weeks, reputedly to protect the fetus from experiencing pain before its ultimate demise. In actuality, fetal pain is a myth, with no grounding in medical science. It was propagated as a tactic to further the anti-abortion agenda to ban all abortions.

Even so, I am always touched by this question. The person sitting in front of me is fully aware that she is ending a potential life, and yet she is deeply concerned for its well-being. I am saddened by the success of the anti-abortion movement for adding guilt and shame to an already difficult decision. To the patient at six weeks, I usually say, "At this stage of pregnancy, it is too early for even the possibility of experiencing pain." Later in pregnancy, it's often the fetal-indication patients who ask about potential fetal pain, and I offer them a longer answer. Their pregnancy is usually highly desired and personified from early on, but they are ending it to spare their child pain and suffering. It only makes sense that these parents are concerned about pain during the abortion process.

"The baby's nervous system gradually develops throughout pregnancy," I tell the group, beginning a full explanation. "Early on, there is a reflex response to any kind of stimulus, whether positive or negative. It is purely a reflex because the pathways to and from the brain—necessary for pain perception—aren't developed yet. For there to be even the possibility of the perception of pain, the nervous system needs to be developed enough for pathways to go from the site of the stimulus to the cortex of the brain. These connections are not intact until at least twenty-four weeks, and further development is necessary for them to be able to function, which occurs at twenty-nine to thirty weeks of gestation. These connections are necessary, but not enough, because to experience pain you also need consciousness."[1]

This raises a complicated question, because the truth is that even scientists don't really know when consciousness occurs. When it comes up, I tell patients that this is almost a philosophical question. I personally believe consciousness occurs at birth. This belief is aligned with my Jewish faith. In Judaism, there is no dogma about abortion. Instead, there are varied opinions and perspectives that have been passed down through the ages. What *is* unquestioned in Judaism is that the woman's life and health take precedence over the fetus during all stages of pregnancy and that health is both physical and mental.

But today I just stick to what I know. I explain to these sad and anxious parents that there is increasing evidence that the intrauterine environment is completely different from the one after birth. Due to the chemical environment in the womb, the fetus is never truly awake but is in a sleeplike unconsciousness. This state suppresses the higher cortical activity necessary to experience pain, and it changes dramatically at birth.

I add: "What I'm telling you are scientific findings, which are important. But your feelings are also important. You are here because you don't want your baby to suffer, and that is one of the reasons we do the injection on the first day, to stop the baby's heartbeat. Now that the heart has stopped, you know there is no longer any possibility of pain."

This explanation seems to be helpful, and the conversation turns back to religion. When I first started this work, I found it interesting that I was caring for so many religious and politically conservative women. By now I realize abortion isn't about religious doctrine, and it isn't about politics. What drives women to have abortions is what they believe they, their families, and their unborn child can handle. It distresses me when a patient's clear-eyed view of their reality conflicts with their religious beliefs. To patients like Mary and Christopher who believe in a harsh and unforgiving god, to have an abortion is to commit an unforgivable sin, and they face the prospect of going to hell for it. For others, like Jamie and Robert, their god is a loving god, who recognizes human frailties and is all-forgiving.

Amrita and Arun have an entirely different perspective. Arun says, "We're Hindu. We believe in reincarnation. This is not a moral issue for us." But believing in reincarnation still did not make this an easy decision for them. Amrita tells the others that the thought of her baby suffering was absolutely intolerable to her.

As the conversation continues, feelings of sadness mixed with anger dance around the room. Why wasn't the anomaly diagnosed earlier? Why the delay? Why did I have to travel to Albuquerque? Why couldn't my doctor take care of me? Why didn't my doctor tell me that abortion was an option? And perhaps the most heartbreaking question: I was a good patient. I am a good person. I would be a good parent. Why did this have to happen to me?

By the time the session draws to a close, the mood in the room has noticeably shifted. What began as a gathering of tense, traumatized people transformed into a room of healing. These people from different states and different backgrounds now seem to deeply understand each other. When they head back to their hotels at the end of the day, my patients are still sad, but they appear calmer and ready to face the next day.

Often at the checkout exam at the end of the week, patients tell me how helpful this group session was for them, even if they'd initially been reluctant to attend and participate. The opportunity to sit in a room with those who understand exactly what they're going through, and to be able to unload all the heavy feelings, is liberating, and not just for the patients. Most often, their partners are also deeply suffering, but men especially often feel the need to bottle their feelings and remain stoic for their partner. These sessions offer catharsis.

Alone in my office at the end of the day, I am drained. Sometimes I feel like I am absorbing the pain of my patients and their partners. I try to get a start on my paperwork but inevitably don't get very far. I'm too tired to eat real food and am content to eat trail mix, a staple of mine for almost twenty years.

Tomorrow I'll start the inductions for the third-trimester patients who are ready. I will also start seeing the first- and second-trimester patients. These will be shorter procedures, but much will be the same. The patients will start with an ultrasound, then have a counseling session. Then I will meet with them, while they are still dressed, and I will connect with them, even if briefly, before we start the abortion.

Tonight, it's unlikely that I'll be called to care for any patients who have gone into labor in the middle of the night, since we just started the cervical preparation today. But it could very well happen the following nights. I should go to bed early, but I'm too wound up thinking about my patients and about potential problems. I'm hoping that Mary's forty-seven-year-old cervix will respond. I'm thinking about Noor's anemia and hoping she won't bleed too much. I'm thinking about Laura's narrow window of reprieve from her husband and how resourceful and brave she is.

I need to clear my mind. I open my laptop and stream a mystery show. I set the alarm for 5:00 a.m., zone out, and fall asleep.

CHAPTER 6

Kansas: 2000s

Kindness, courtesy, justice, love, and
respect are the overarching principles of
the doctor/patient relationship.

—GEORGE R. TILLER, MD

In 2000, it was with a tremendous sense of relief and excitement
that I ended my career as a generalist ob-gyn, leaving behind my
frustrations and disappointments in the field. Now in my forties,
I was starting afresh, exclusively providing abortion care—work I
believed in wholeheartedly.

I took the advice of the medical director at a local Planned
Parenthood who recommended that, to gain as much experience as
possible, I work in as many different clinics as I could. My first year
I worked at two different Planned Parenthood affiliates in the Bay
Area, traveling from clinic to clinic to provide first- and second-
trimester abortions. The cases were no-frills abortion procedures,
functional and basic. But they were exactly what I needed to help
me gain the skills of the specialty.

It didn't take long, however, before I began to long for the one-
on-one patient connections I'd cherished since first volunteering at
the community clinic in Madison. The Planned Parenthood clinics were designed to provide an essential service: Women walked
in with an undesired pregnancy, and, when they left, they were
safe and no longer pregnant. That was paramount. But there was

little slack in the schedule, and the organization had a top-down structure, with relatively little autonomy for local affiliates, clinics, and providers.

Throughout this year, I kept thinking of Dr. McMahon's clinic. I knew a different level of emotional care was possible in the abortion setting, if only I could find it again.

In September 2001, while I was still working in local California clinics, I attended one of my first meetings of the National Abortion Federation (NAF), the professional association of abortion providers. I knew almost no one, but I went.

In the Toronto convention center, I walked the full floor of the exhibition hall, taking in every display and presentation. Just outside the main hall, in a corner, I discovered a booth run by Dr. George Tiller, the renowned provider of third-trimester abortion care. He was screening a silent video of his technique. As the video ran, Dr. Tiller stood next to the screen speaking about his approach. He was reciting the same basic aphorisms that I later found out he repeated on almost a daily basis to his patients and staff: "Four rules of the practice: A woman's body is smarter than the doctor. Time, patience, and the baby will come. Respect the woman's rhythm. And if you forget the second and third, remember the first: A woman's body is smarter than the doctor."

"That's midwifery," I piped up.

Seemingly intrigued, Dr. Tiller began to pepper me with questions. What did I know about midwifery? Where had I trained? Where was I working? Was I married? What did my husband do? I answered each question in turn, and when I told him that my husband was a wife, he responded evenly, "That's okay, that's okay." I had the feeling he wasn't expecting that answer and was responding in the best way that he could.

Within five minutes, he offered me a job. He invited me to spend a week at his clinic, Women's Health Care Services, in Wichita, Kansas. I thought it very strange to get a job offer so quickly; that had never happened before. But I was interested. Here was a doctor offering the type of abortion care I could support. I decided to

accept the invitation to visit. Soon afterward, I received the first
of many letters from him:

> [I] wanted to get some of my thoughts down on paper immedi-
> ately, because I think that you and I are not terribly dissimilar in
> our approach to patients in the healthcare realms in which we
> endeavor.
>
> Your interest in my practice and Women's Health Care Ser-
> vices is greatly appreciated. As I said, when I looked at your re-
> sume, I thought that you and I should be emotionally, spiritually,
> perhaps culturally and philosophically in at least the same ball
> park in our approach to patients. Since we seem to agree on this
> and, of course, I think philosophical, emotional, spiritual and
> cultural harmony is extremely important in the development of a
> compatible relationship, we can move forward . . .
>
> Thank you again for your interest in Women's Health Care
> Services and our practice. Again, if we are emotionally, spiritu-
> ally and philosophically motivated in similar patient care ori-
> entation, we can make the details of this proposed association
> work out in a win for me, for my facility, for my staff, for you,
> your professional life, and for your partner and family. I think we
> should try to work toward a six-way win.

The letter was formal and a little awkward, but also earnest and
heartfelt. That was Dr. Tiller's style, I would learn, and it appealed
to me. I liked the idea of being "emotionally, spiritually, perhaps
culturally and philosophically in at least the same ball park." As at
Eve's, where even the design of the entryway path was considered,
I could already sense that patients' needs at Dr. Tiller's clinic were
attended to well beyond ending their pregnancies.

Before I arranged my trip, I did a little research on Dr. Tiller. I
learned that his father, Dr. Jack Tiller, had been a well-known family medicine doctor in Wichita and that George Tiller had followed
in his footsteps by becoming a physician. In 1970, however, Dr.
Jack, as he was known, was killed in a plane crash, along with his

wife, daughter, and son-in-law. George Tiller was then working as a naval flight surgeon in California and planning to begin residency in dermatology. Instead, he abandoned his dermatology dreams, moved back to Wichita, and took over his father's family practice.

At first, Dr. Tiller worked exclusively as a family physician. But over time, unhappily pregnant women came to see him and asked him to help them "the way your father used to." The first time this happened, he angrily turned the woman away. He was horrified that he would be asked to perform what was then an illegal abortion. He had no idea that his father had provided them to his patients. However, when the requests continued even after the *Roe* decision legalizing abortion, he had a change of heart and began to offer abortion care himself. Eventually, the abortion practice became so busy that he closed the family practice and focused exclusively on abortion care. Like Dr. McMahon, he developed a technique for providing third-trimester abortions, and, in time, this made him a focal point for anti-abortion protestors.

I hadn't known about the 1991 Summer of Mercy, but now I learned. That was the summer when the anti-abortion group Operation Rescue descended on Wichita with thousands of protestors intent on shutting down Dr. Tiller's clinic. Initially, their leader, Keith Tucci, called for a one-week nonviolent protest. To prevent mayhem and violence, Dr. Tiller, along with the directors of the two other local abortion clinics, reached an agreement with local police to close their clinics for that week. However, rather than tamping down the anti-abortion activists' fervor, their success in closing the clinics that week only emboldened them. Tucci decided to extend the protest to six weeks, culminating in a massive rally attended by over twenty-five thousand. Dr. Tiller felt betrayed and was determined never to agree to close the clinic again.

During those six weeks, there were almost daily protests outside the clinic, with protestors blocking the entrance to the clinic and chaining themselves to the clinic door. All told, local police arrested over 2,600 protestors. Signaling his approval of the protestors, President George H. W. Bush dispatched then–Department of Justice lawyer and current Supreme Court Chief Justice John Roberts to Wichita to argue *against* a federal judge's order restraining the protestors' actions. Eventually, the dispute led to the 1994 passage of the Freedom of Access to Clinic Entrances (FACE) Act under President Clinton, which made blocking clinic entrances a federal crime. But the scale of the 1991 protests ultimately galvanized the national anti-abortion movement, and it emboldened extremist activists.

Not long after, in 1993, a woman named Shelley Shannon attempted to kill Dr. Tiller. In fact, she narrowly missed shooting him through the heart. It was only because he raised his right arm to give her the finger when she approached him that the bullet struck his arm rather than his chest. Shannon was sentenced to eleven years for attempted murder, then another twenty years for six firebombings and acid attacks on abortion clinics in Oregon, California, and Nevada. Dr. Tiller, for his part, went right back to work. The bullet had only grazed his arm, and, defiantly, he returned to the clinic the next day.

Before meeting Dr. Tiller, I knew almost nothing about him or his history. In 1991, when the Summer of Mercy chaos was happening, I was an ob-gyn resident who thought of nothing beyond work and sleep. In 1993, when Shelley Shannon shot Dr. Tiller, I had just finished training and was insulated from the political realities of abortion care. I had only ever been to Kansas to visit Julie's mother in Topeka. And since I had only provided abortion care in California, I could hardly imagine the embattled environment of Wichita.

It turned out that I met Dr. Tiller at an opportune moment. He was ready to train his successor, and I was in search of a mentor. In October 2001, I accepted Dr. Tiller's offer to visit, and I arranged to spend a week at his clinic in Wichita. During that week, I was able to see Dr. Tiller's third-trimester abortion process from beginning to end, from Tuesday to Saturday. It was a multiday process that synthesized technical and emotional care, and it became the model for my own later practice in Albuquerque.

I arrived in Wichita on a Monday evening and checked into the local La Quinta hotel, five minutes away from the clinic. This was where all the third-trimester patients were advised to stay, and the on-call nurse stayed there as well. That way, if a patient went into labor in the middle of the night, the on-call nurse was able to quickly bring the patient to the clinic for care.

The next morning, Dr. Tiller, dressed in his Tuesday suit, pulled up to the La Quinta hotel in a big four-door jeep that looked as sturdy as a tank. I later learned that it was custom built for him after he survived the first assassination attempt. It was outfitted with bulletproof windows, and the doors were so heavy that they sagged.

Dr. Tiller drove me to the clinic, and as we approached, I saw that it was surrounded by big wooden fences. Protestors stood outside the fences on a small strip of grass and sidewalk that was public property. They were forbidden to go past the fences into the parking lot, since that was private property. Still, the protestors felt completely emboldened to approach cars and harass the drivers and passengers as they drove into the parking lot. (Once, years later, a patient's husband, not a native English speaker, told me he couldn't understand what they wanted and thought they were offering valet parking. Wisely, he didn't hand over his keys.)

As we parked and walked up to the clinic, I noticed a large American flag in the parking lot, something I had never seen at an abortion clinic before. I came to understand that Dr. Tiller was deeply patriotic, stemming from his beliefs in what he perceived to be core American values: freedom, democracy, and justice. It was his patriotism that led him each year to offer free first-trimester abortions on July 4th and to send American flags as gifts to his colleagues in abortion care throughout the country.

There was a security guard at the entrance and a metal detector everyone had to go through. Past the detector and the administrative office, we came into a large waiting room for patients and their support people. The walls were filled with framed patient letters of gratitude, and I also noticed a blown-up photograph of Dr. Tiller shaking hands with then-president Bill Clinton. By now, we were well into the George W. Bush years, and I knew I would never see a photo of Dr. Tiller with the current president.

Dr. Tiller began a tour of the clinic, guiding me to a separate waiting room that was devoted to the fetal-indication patients. Dr. Tiller's practice of grouping patients into maternal indications and fetal indications cohorts inspired my own. He recognized that their reasons and emotions surrounding abortion were often distinct, and he wanted to treat them accordingly. The walls in this room were covered with framed letters specifically from former fetal-indication patients from around the world. The purpose of displaying these letters was to help current patients gain reassurance from those who had come before them with similar stories.

To the left of the large waiting room was a door that could be locked from the inside, which led to the clinical side of the practice. Inside were three small procedure rooms for first-trimester abortions, while second-trimester abortions were performed in one of two operating rooms in the back of the clinic. First- and second-trimester procedures occurred on Wednesdays, Thursdays, and Fridays.

Tuesdays were reserved for meeting the third-trimester patients. This day was deliberately designed with two goals in mind: to begin the technical abortion procedure and to initiate the emotionally therapeutic part of the abortion. The format was much like the one I later used in New Mexico: filling out paperwork, an ultrasound, and basic lab work. A video of Dr. Tiller explaining the abortion process was followed by either Dr. Tiller or a nurse answering questions and an introduction to the on-staff clergy.

Finally, Dr. Tiller met each patient individually, along with their partners or parents. He addressed their concerns and answered questions until the patients were ready to sign consent forms. I immediately noted the respect that Dr. Tiller showed his patients and how he put patients at ease. Dr. Tiller always wore a well-cut suit on Tuesdays—he didn't think wearing scrubs would make the best first impression. And he took the time to assuage all the fear and anxiety patients had brought with them into the clinic.

After all the meetings had been completed, patients moved to one of the procedure rooms, where Dr. Tiller began the first steps in the multiday abortion process. Afterward came group sessions—the same schedule I would adopt and adapt in my subsequent practice.

The procedure Dr. Tiller performed in Wichita was the induction of labor and the delivery of a stillborn. During labor, which happened later in the week, Dr. Tiller used medications—a narcotic and a sedative—to induce twilight sleep, a variant of an early twentieth-century childbirth technique. Patients were awake with contractions and then fell asleep between contractions. They often had little memory of the laboring process. Due to the heavy use of medications, they mainly lay flat or on their sides until they were ready to deliver.

This was a very different technique from the one I had observed at Dr. McMahon's Eve clinic. Dr. McMahon had used medication and mechanical dilation to open the woman's cervix to a specific and desired dilation. At that point, he extracted the fetus with instruments, using the intact D&X procedure. In contrast, at Women's Health Care Services, as long as the process was going smoothly, the patient delivered a premature stillborn. Dr. Tiller saw this as a much more "natural" way of ending a pregnancy.

As he continued the tour, our next stop was the space where labor took place: gurney, a large room filled with gurney beds separated by curtains. The deliveries either took place in this room, in bathrooms with handles to optimize pushing efforts, or in the operating room. There were two to three clinic workers assigned to gurney whose role was to assess the patients' well-being, administer medication, and assist with the delivery process. As with my later practice, these deliveries took place at their own pace, occurring anytime between Thursday and Saturday.

Next was the quiet room. Here, there were no patient letters on the walls. This was a contemplative, peaceful space where, if they requested, patients and their support people viewed the baby after the delivery. This was the room that became the province of Reverend George Gardner. A former pastor of Wichita's College Hill United Methodist Church, George Gardner was representative of a church that supported, rather than condemned, those making the decision to end a pregnancy.

Reverend George Gardner initiated and developed the chaplaincy program at Dr. Tiller's clinic, which aimed to speak to "the many emotional and spiritual concerns that surround the choice of abortion."[1] For those who requested it, Reverend Gardner said a prayer and baptized the baby with holy water. For others, he tailored his approach to their own faith or lack thereof, offering an approach that was respectful of all religious and spiritual beliefs.

Aside from conducting the viewings, Reverend Gardner practiced what he called "ministry while walking around." Always dressed with his clerical collar, he walked around the clinic waiting room making himself available to anyone—patient, family, or accompanying friend—who wanted to chat. Sometimes, he just sat and held a hand. He exemplified the healing potential of the "power of presence," a term mainly used in midwifery circles but applicable to religious circles as well. A calm, reassuring presence could often be more effective than any words or actions. Although Reverend Gardner succumbed to cancer in 2004, the clinic continued to use the services of clergy, who were integral in relieving patients' and families' spiritual distress.

During my visit to Wichita, I came to admire Dr. Tiller and his approach, but I was equally impressed by the people he worked with. Reverend Gardner was just one of the many staff members at Dr. Tiller's clinic who were warm, open, and friendly. While the staff in the California clinics where I worked were often young reproductive rights activists—short-term employees on their way to careers as doctors, nurse practitioners, and therapists—the Women's Health Care Services staff saw their clinic work as a long-term career. Working at WHCS required fortitude, commitment, and the ability to withstand the attacks the clinic faced almost daily. Dr. Tiller recognized the importance of having a cohesive staff, and he valued and appreciated each employee. He often organized events and activities that involved the full staff. In addition to an annual bonus, employees received a gift for every five years of service to the clinic—ranging from an expensive watch to a vacation in Hawaii or even a down payment on a house.

One night, before I returned to California, Dr. Tiller brought me to his country club to meet his wife, Jeanne, and get what he called "the eyeball test" from her, an opportunity for her to see me and talk with me. Although she was not intimately involved in the clinic, he valued her opinion and wanted to make sure she could connect with me before he made the decision to hire me.

He also gave me some "homework," asking me to write down my goals and aspirations, both familial and occupational. All these years later, I still hold onto the notepad where I set down those early career goals. Leafing back through them, I find my old aspirations and smile to myself, remembering the care I took in writing these out for Dr. Tiller that first week. These were my occupational goals:

- to increase my technical expertise
- to be an excellent abortion provider
- to be in a setting where people are committed to their work and where I am appreciated, and where I appreciate my co-workers
- to have a mentor

I was sure after visiting that Dr. Tiller's clinic was the right place for me. In fact, I felt it from the moment I first walked through the doors. The place embodied what Dr. Tiller often said were the cornerstones of good patient care: kindness, courtesy, justice, love, and respect. Dr. Tiller had told me he was beginning to think of retirement and was looking for someone to train and eventually take over his practice. I, in turn, felt that this was a place where I could find the mentor I was looking for. I could perfect my technical abortion skills and, more importantly, practice in a setting that valued the patient's physical *and* emotional well-being.

Soon after I arrived home, Dr. Tiller invited me to join the practice. This was a once-in-a-lifetime opportunity for me, but not for my wife, Julie, or our five-year-old son, NoahLani. As thrilled as I was by the job offer, Julie was concerned. Moving to Kansas, a place Julie had left years ago, was not an option. The only way this opportunity could work was for me to "commute" to Wichita from California. In this scenario, I would be gone from home for one week out of every two to three weeks, which meant that Julie would be a single mother for large chunks of time.

We went to therapy to help talk it through. The therapist told us that, in her experience, relationships didn't last long when one partner consistently travelled out of town. Usually, either the relationship broke apart or the travelling partner stayed home and gave up whatever compelled them to travel. Friends were dubious as well. But, despite her hesitations, Julie agreed to let me follow my dream and passion. And we proved everyone wrong.

I told Dr. Tiller I was willing to join if I could spend a week in Wichita followed by two weeks back in California, then repeat. He knew I was not going to work every day; we had agreed from our first discussions that I would be there part time. But he had hoped for me to be in Kansas working in the clinic a few days a week every week. When I told him the travel schedule that I could manage, he grew uncertain. His biggest fear was that he would teach me everything he knew and that I would then open a clinic in California and compete with him. It took another round of negotiations to convince him I had *no* desire to open or manage a clinic. Indeed, my biggest fear was that I wouldn't have the chance to work with him.

Eventually, we compromised. For the first six months, I would travel from Oakland every other week, and, later, I would work one week out of three. After months of circling each other, we finally figured out a way to work together.

I started at the clinic in June 2002. When I performed my first abortion, Dr. Tiller's joy was palpable. I treated a patient at twelve weeks' gestation, toward the end of the first trimester, and after watching me, George exclaimed, "Yes! She's good!" We had spent months going back and forth making sure I was the right fit and that the schedule could work. But Dr. Tiller had hired me without knowing anything about my skills. There was quite a bit of relief on both sides.

Still, the beginning of our relationship was challenging. Even though we knew our goals and values were in the same place, we just did not understand each other on a personal level. I found him to be prickly, and he thought I was obstinate, which led to a lot of early miscommunication. But we both persisted. Whenever there was an issue between us, George would say, "This is not an event, this is a relationship," which I interpreted to mean: let's keep working on this because we're in it for the long haul.

As time passed, he proved right, and we became close. Early on, George took me to a show at a local theater and introduced me effusively to several friends. "I'm proud of myself for hiring you," he explained to me afterward. Despite our initial communication problems, we realized that we not only got along but that we also enjoyed each other's company. I appreciated his dry sense of humor and occasional sarcasm.

Training and working with George was like a dream come true. I loved his meticulous attention to detail in both the technical and the emotional aspects of the work. I loved his astute psychological insight into our patients and how he was able to establish connections with them. I loved sitting with him in his office and listening as he talked to patients, and I loved talking with him. He was an excellent teacher who became a wonderful colleague and friend.

Working with George was akin to working with my midwife mentor, Kate. He improved my first- and second-trimester abortion skills and taught me the technical skills for third-trimester abortions, but these were just one part of the learning process. The hours and hours that I spent at George's side as he talked to patients were just as important, if not more so.

By the time I met George, I had been providing abortions very sporadically for seven years, then consistently for fewer than two. I thought, with the hubris of the inexperienced, that I knew what I was doing. But my previous training had been haphazard, and my technique needed refining. Under George's tutelage, I started from the very beginning, perfecting my first-trimester abortion technique; then I gradually worked my way up to second-trimester abortions.

George was a meticulous teacher. His abortion technique was like his personality: gentle, patient, and thorough. This approach resonated with me. At first, he stood by my side, watching me. Following the abortion, we talked about it, with him noting every little nuance, including how I held the instruments and how I sat in my chair. He could sense when I got frustrated or felt uncertain, and afterward, he told me about the destructive power of negative self-talk, which he had learned to redirect to positive self-talk. I wasn't always successful in redirection, but I did come up with what I called a "tactical retreat." Sometimes that meant that if I felt stuck and the patient was stable during a first- or second-trimester abortion, I would stop to take a few breaths before restarting the procedure. Sometimes it meant stepping out of the room for a moment. In the third trimester, if labor was not progressing, that might mean pausing for some hours and then restarting, rather than pushing ahead.

Once I started working in Kansas, I had the chance to meet and appreciate two other doctors who worked part time with Dr. Tiller. Dr. Norman Harris was a retired ob-gyn from Salina, Kansas, who assisted with first- and second-trimester patients and covered the practice when George was out of town. He was an old-school ob-gyn who taught George about labor and, crucially, taught him that knowing when to stand back and allow the natural process of labor to unfold was as important as knowing when to intervene. The other doctor at the time was Dr. Lee Carhart. He travelled from his abortion clinic in Bellevue, Nebraska, to assist Dr. Tiller with first- and second-trimester abortions. Once I was hired, he worked on my off weeks and eventually joined the third-trimester practice.

The nurses at the practice were equally essential. Cathy Reavis, the lead nurse, was Dr. Tiller's right-hand woman. She supervised the medical staff, and she knew everything about the clinic. Cathy was the person I learned to approach whenever I faced a patient dilemma while Dr. Tiller was away. I could ask her, "What would Dr. Tiller do?" and she would know the answer. She had the heart of a midwife, and she believed wholeheartedly in the birthing process. Time and time again, I would hear her give encouragement to scared patients: "Women are designed to have eight-to-nine-pound babies. This pregnancy is a lot smaller. You can do this!"

JoAn (pronounced Joanne) Armentrout was the clinic's administrative director. JoAn had been hired as a bookkeeper years prior, but Dr. Tiller saw her potential and encouraged her. She had grown up in small-town Kansas and viscerally understood the clinic's mission. Pregnant at sixteen and before abortion was legal, she was forced to continue the pregnancy, drop out of high school, and marry her abusive boyfriend. The guilt and shame she felt as a pregnant teenager persisted as an abused woman, but eventually, she sought legal help and filed for divorce. At that point, she was a single mother in the mid-1960s, barely scraping by. But she studied for her GED and subsequently remarried a much kinder man, with whom she had another child. Meanwhile, she taught herself accounting and worked in a series of motorcycle dealerships as a bookkeeper before answering an ad for a job at WHCS. For years, Dr. Tiller asked her to be the administrative director, but lacking self-confidence, she turned him down. He told her he would keep asking until she agreed, which she finally did. When she agreed, he promised to buy her a motorcycle if she stayed until she was seventy-two years old.

Both JoAn and Cathy were about fifteen years older than I was, and they seemed much wiser. I admired their strength, courage, and wisdom, and during the years I worked in Kansas, I learned a great deal from them.

Aside from the few weeks I had spent with Jim McMahon, I joined Dr. Tiller's clinic knowing little about third-trimester abortion care. Here I was a true beginner. George always said that the technical part of the procedure—the premature delivery of a stillborn—was simple. What was complicated was the emotional component. I thought that both had their challenges.

To learn these skills, I spent untold hours by George's side as he cared for patients. He was a careful listener and picked up on the subtlest cues patients transmitted. He spoke calmly and never appeared rushed. Patients felt cared for by him and the staff and often said this was the best healthcare they had ever received. And I understood what they meant. The clinic did not just attend to patients' physical needs to end the pregnancy. Dr. Tiller and the staff were also paying scrupulous attention to their emotional and spiritual needs. This approach resonated deeply with me.

Dr. Tiller had an openness and humility that was disarming. He met an openly trans person who I cared for at his clinic. This was years ago, before there was much trans awareness. George brought him to his office and gently said, "Tell me how I should address you. I'm not familiar with this." The patient's tense shoulders softened, and he and Dr. Tiller began to talk.

George also had an unflagging belief in the birth process. At times, when labor seemed to drag and delivery seemed to be a distant reality, it was easy for me to become discouraged. George would say, "Time, patience, and the baby will come." And it always did. This was a mantra that I repeated to myself and to the staff many times over the years. It was an axiom that never disappointed.

As the years went by, our relationship deepened. I often thought of George as the iconic American hero from the 1950s—a white Christian churchgoer, tall, taciturn, honest, who gets the job done without any self-aggrandizement. Think Gary Cooper.

Unfortunately, most of the world didn't agree with my assessment. On his Fox News show *The O'Reilly Factor*, Bill O'Reilly, Tucker Carlson's ideological father, endlessly labeled George "Tiller the Killer."

The attacks against George were never-ending and lodged on many fronts. Around the country, the aim of anti-abortion activists was to vilify, discredit, and bankrupt providers through harassment. They tied them up with frivolous yet expensive lawsuits, with the ultimate goal of closing clinics. In a novel tactic in Kansas, the anti-abortion group Operation Rescue exploited a law dating back to 1887 allowing citizens to call for grand jury investigations, which added yet another battleground.

In the seven years I was with WHCS, George was subject to one grand jury investigation, one criminal case, and multiple investigations by three attorneys general. He was eventually absolved in all of them, but at great monetary and emotional expense. There were multiple complaints to the Kansas State Board of Healing Arts (the Kansas medical board), lodged either directly by Operation Rescue or by former patients who had come under their sway. The board pursued all these complaints, no matter how trivial.

I was the target of several board investigations as well. In 2008, Operation Rescue lodged a complaint accusing me of murder, alleging that a fetus had been born alive and that I killed it after delivery. In this case, in addition to the medical board complaint, Operation Rescue reported me to the Wichita Police Department, urging them to launch a murder investigation. I could easily refute this accusation by going back to the medical chart where my notes, as in all cases, recorded that I had done an ultrasound days before the delivery, confirming that the fetus had already died. The case was closed without action after an investigation. Yet given how inflammatory the charge was, it continues to live on the internet.

Other cases were more complicated. There was the case of Michelle, for instance. (I have not changed her name as this case, including Michelle's name, is on anti-abortion websites.) Michelle was an eighteen-year-old young woman who came to the clinic accompanied by her mother. Michelle appeared sure in her decision, with no signs of ambivalence. After we spoke, she signed consents, and I began the abortion process. She returned to her hotel with her mother and planned to come back to the clinic the next morning, when we would continue to prepare her body for the eventual induction and delivery.

That evening, her boyfriend came to her hotel room and unsuccessfully tried to convince Michelle to change her mind and continue the pregnancy. Michelle returned to the clinic to continue the abortion, and the rest of her time at the clinic was uneventful. At her checkout exam, she said she had no regrets and felt relieved.

Years later, her life circumstances had dramatically changed, and her feelings about the abortion had changed. She had married the boyfriend and went on to have three children with him. She now believed that she had only agreed to have an abortion because of pressure from her parents. Accompanied by Operation Rescue, she testified in front of the Kansas State Legislature about her abortion. Operation Rescue filed a politically motivated complaint against me on her behalf, consisting of fourteen allegations. The most serious allegation was that I proceeded with the abortion without seeing or speaking to her beforehand. She also charged that I didn't pressure her *not* to have an abortion. Finally, the complaint alleged that: "The minister from the Unity Church [Reverend George Gardner] who spoke with her as a part of the 'counseling' at WHCS fraudulently represented to her that the Catholic Church allows for abortion. The patient was a recent convert to Catholicism and alleged that the minister of WHCS had misrepresented the teachings of the Catholic Church on abortion. She said that this counseling was unethical and fraudulent, and caused the patient emotional pain."[2]

The Board did not find any of the allegations valid but instructed me to update my recordkeeping practice. While these complaints may seem trivial and were invariably resolved favorably, they were always hanging over us. I saw Michelle in 2003, but the whole issue wasn't completely resolved until May 13, 2009.

We were always either under attack or under investigation and, often, both at the same time. One 2004 attack by Operation Rescue failed miserably. Designed to harass and intimidate staff and to convince them to quit working at the clinic, Operation Rescue began flooding their neighborhoods with anti-abortion flyers and sending their neighbors postcards, "outing" them as employees of WHCS. Operation Rescue activists also followed and harassed staff members when they were out running errands or going out to eat. The idea was that even if Dr. Tiller was resolute in keeping the clinic open, it would be impossible to stay open if his staff quit.

The campaign moved westward to the Bay Area, and my neighbors received multiple postcards in their mailboxes. One particularly gruesome card had a photo of a dismembered fetus, with the words: "IT'S NOT PRETTY. IT'S NOT NICE. IT'S ABORTION. AND IT'S WHAT YOUR NEIGHBOR, SHELLY [sic] IS DOING THIS WEEK, DECEMBER 1–3 IN WICHITA, KS." Another pictured a cartoon of a girl, presumably me, holding a vacuum cleaner up to a doll—the girl stands next to a boy in sneakers and a backward-facing cap. The bubble above the girl/me said: "LET'S PLAY DOCTOR. I'LL SUCK HER BRAINS OUT. YOU CRUSH HER SKULL."

Operation Rescue also operated a truck with huge photos of dismembered fetuses on its side that it called the Truth Truck. George called it the Trash Truck. One day the group's members drove the truck through my neighborhood in Oakland, dropping off leaflets and posters. "Shelley Sella is an ABORTIONIST," the poster said, with my address below. I wasn't home when they drove by my block, but I heard that my neighbor cursed the driver of the truck loudly and heartily. The driver apparently got the message and never returned.

Rather than rebuking me, my neighbors sent me letters and cards of support. A typical one said: "We want you to know that this neighborhood is not filled with hate. So sorry that you're having to endure this hateful campaign. Your neighbors." An acquaintance from San Francisco wrote: "I had no idea that Shelley had such an awesome job! Keep up the good work and know that you have our love and support during this difficult time."

The postcard campaign also backfired in Kansas. In Wichita, even neighbors who might have been anti-abortion were affronted by this invasion of privacy. Heartened by their neighbors' responses, none of the staff quit.

While Operation Rescue waged its campaigns, the conservative Kansas State Legislature proceeded with its own. Year after year it passed one anti-abortion bill after another, including a parental consent law and a twenty-four-hour waiting period, which required women to wait twenty-four hours after receiving counseling and giving their consent before the abortion procedure could be performed. When an anti-abortion state legislator found herself pregnant, she asked George to waive the twenty-four-hour waiting period for her. After all, she had to get back to the important work of passing more anti-abortion legislation. George told her that she had supported that bill so she should adhere to it, and he sent her away, as was now mandated by law.

Over time, members of the medical community became afraid to support George publicly, although they continued to refer patients to him. On the rare occasions when there was a complication and a patient had to be transferred to the hospital, hospital staff approached me and surreptitiously whispered that they supported our work.

The business community, under pressure and threat of boycott by anti-abortion groups, also abandoned George. The waste management company severed our contract. The La Quinta hotel, where patients had stayed for years, requested that they not be referred to stay there any longer. FedEx called the clinic director, saying that its drivers were getting harassed by the protestors and asked whether we could pick up our packages at a different location. The owner of a local cab company was a friend of George's, but when the company was taken over by a larger one, the new owner refused to pick up our patients to drive them to and from the clinic. One day when I flew into Wichita, I tried to hail a cab from the airport to the clinic.

Driver one wouldn't take me.

Driver two wouldn't take me.

Driver three, a male, asked, "Are you going to perform an abortion?"

"Well, certainly not on you," I responded, and he drove away.

No luck with driver four.

Finally, driver five—Farah,* a Muslim convert whose grandfather was a Southern Baptist minister and who had driven me before—agreed, and off we went.

The daily harassment outside the clinic would never have been tolerated at any other business, but it was condoned by the police and public officials. Every morning, the Trash Truck was parked outside, and rows of protestors settled in for a day of shouting. Sometimes, a sickle-wielding man walked up and down the block. One day, police were called about the noise from a man with a bullhorn outside the clinic yelling, "Daddy, daddy, don't kill your baby." The city attorney responded, "Well, you are just going to have to get used to it because I'd rather be sued by Tiller than Operation Rescue." Operation Rescue and its anti-abortion supporters managed to intimidate an entire community. Or maybe the community had gotten tired of the controversy and were happy to have Operation Rescue do their dirty work for them.

Despite all the attacks and intimidation, we kept doing our work. But the atmosphere outside felt heavier and heavier. It didn't seem like things were ever going to get better.

---

* Pseudonym

CHAPTER 7

Wednesday

I don't think I've felt this much peace of mind in a
long time. Even though I'm really physically tired,
emotionally, it makes up for everything else.

—ANONYMOUS PATIENT

Birth can be overwhelming, scary, and even terrifying. It is challenging and often difficult, and yet, it can also be a beautiful and
a profoundly spiritual experience. A midwife's role is to guide and
support the woman, to create an environment where the patient
has control. This was also my role as a provider of third-trimester
abortion care, even though the outcome was not a live birth.

In my abortion practice, time was compressed. The staff and
I did not have months to get to know patients; we had days. And
yet, like the home birth midwives I worked with, our aim was to
create a supportive environment, one that engendered trust in us,
and trust and belief in the patients' innate abilities to deliver. In
my practice, I hoped that the experience would be an empowering
one, as I knew that many of my patients wanted to give birth and
raise children in the future. I was gratified when a patient told me,
"Even though it was an abortion, it was still an experience. Giving
birth is a beautiful thing."

The patients were in our care for a week, and by the end of it,
when our patients were no longer pregnant, I wanted them to feel
confident in their abilities to overcome any future challenges that
they might face. I also wanted them to feel powerful and positive
about what they had undergone. When a patient told me, describing

her experience, "It felt so beautiful coming out. All this hard work and I'm free!" I knew that the deep roots of midwifery and my seven years with Dr. Tiller had taken hold.

I'm back at the clinic after my 5:30 a.m. swim. Today, I'll start caring for first- and second-trimester patients, in addition to those in the third trimester who I met yesterday. All of the first-trimester patients and the earlier second-trimester patients, those up to twenty weeks, will be completed in one day. The procedures for the later second-trimester patients, through twenty-three weeks, will take two days. I'll start preparing their cervices today and complete their abortions tomorrow, Thursday.

Before the first- and second-trimester patients start arriving, however, I'll check the third-trimester patients. First, I will check the patients I think will be induced today based on yesterday's exams—Amrita, Jamie, and Laura. They have already received their first dose of misoprostol, one pill in each cheek, the pill that will help soften and shorten the cervix and will start labor. The pill will gradually dissolve and will be repeated every two hours until they deliver.

After I remove the laminaria, the sterile dilators I inserted yesterday, I examine Jamie's cervix, which has already shortened significantly and is starting to open. I break the bag of water, the fluid surrounding the baby, to help the baby descend and press against the cervix, which helps it dilate. I have the counselor bring her to gurney, the laboring room, where most patients deliver. I do the same for Amrita and Laura, as their cervices also feel ready for induction today.

As I leave Laura's room, a counselor approaches and tells me that Mary just arrived and seems to be very uncomfortable. That's surprising. Given her age of forty-seven and the fact that she has never given birth before, I expected that it would take time for her body to go into labor and that today I would need to reinsert laminaria and begin the induction on Thursday. I ask that she be put in an exam room to be checked as soon as possible.

I hear the moans of labor as Mary is taken to a room. She tells me that she had mild, manageable cramping overnight that has become more intense over the last few hours. I take out the laminaria, check her cervix, and am amazed to feel the baby starting to come through the cervix. (As I had explained to the group in the meeting yesterday, at this stage of pregnancy, it's normal for the cervix not to be completely dilated at delivery.) This is the patient whose cervix I was most worried about. Once again, I'm reminded of the unpredictability of labor, either in a third-trimester abortion or in a live birth at term.

Mary is so close to delivering that I keep her in the exam room rather than escort her to gurney. With a counselor at her side murmuring encouragement, Mary gives a loud howl and quickly delivers. I cut the umbilical cord, take the baby, wrap him in a drape sheet, and bring him to the lab, where he will be washed and prepared for the viewing that Mary and Christopher requested. The placenta, attached to the uterus, separates on its own and comes out. Then, under ultrasound guidance, I perform a D&C, the dilation and curettage to empty the uterus of any fluid and to check for excessive bleeding. Mary is bleeding lightly, which is normal after a delivery, and she is doing well. When she is ready, she goes to the recovery room and rests under the watchful eyes of the recovery room nurse.

Ordinarily, Christopher would have been in the room while Mary delivered, but it all happened so quickly that he was left sitting in the waiting room. A counselor lets him know that all's well and that she'll bring him to the private area of the recovery room, which we call the annex, to sit with Mary as she recovers over the next two hours.

Now, instead of three, there are only two patients, Irene and Noor, waiting for reinsertion of laminaria. Both of their cervices have changed overnight. Although they are not ready to induce today, their cervices are starting to soften, shorten, and open. I anticipate that they will be ready to induce tomorrow.

After I have checked Noor and placed a new set of laminaria, I have a few free moments before the other patients are ready to be seen, and I decide to check in with her father, Kareem. We sit down to talk in the counseling room, where he pours out feelings that he suppressed when I met him together with Noor on Tuesday. He is worried about Noor and worried what others will think. He plaintively asks, "How could this happen? We watch her so carefully. How could Noor do this to us? If she had had this baby, she would have brought shame upon us. She would have been ostracized by our community. She wouldn't have been able to pursue a career. Who will marry her now that she's not a virgin?" Then, he takes a few breaths and slows down. He tells me how much he loves his daughter and how proud he is of her. As hard as this time has been for him and his wife since finding out she was pregnant, they are glad that they can help her. I mostly just listen, gratified that he has an opportunity to talk to someone who understands and will judge neither him nor his daughter. When we are done and I get up to leave, he tells me as much.

By the time I talk to Kareem, I have talked to many parents. I understand how their deep love for their daughters led them to bring their child to an abortion clinic—like so many patients and parents, a place they never thought they would be. After our initial meeting on the first day, I always try to find time later in the week to speak privately with parents of girls and teenagers. It never takes much to start the conversation. I bring the parent(s) into a counseling room and ask the simple question "How are you doing?" That's often all it takes to unleash the feelings and questions they have been holding inside since they found out their daughter was pregnant and wanted an abortion. Once they arrive at the clinic, they are usually stoic in front of their daughters. They need to be strong. Alone in a safe space, it is a different story.

Many, many tears are shed. This is when parents tell me about their bewilderment that their daughter couldn't disclose that she was pregnant. "How could we not have known? How could we not have seen that she was pregnant?" Mothers often say, "We have always been so close. She tells me everything. Why didn't she feel that she could talk to me earlier? I asked her so many times if she could be pregnant and she kept saying no."

They often say that they wish they could take on the pain their daughter is going through—as if they haven't already. They tell me about their love for their daughter and the sacrifices they have made; for example, working two jobs to support her and provide her with opportunities they never had.

Often, these girls are top students or athletes, and they know how proud their parents are of them. We talk about the fear their daughters have of disappointing or angering them, of bringing shame to their family. How could they violate their parents' trust and belief in them? Although they invariably need their parents' help to get an abortion, they are too afraid to say anything until late in the pregnancy. And sometimes, they never say anything, like Noor—and it is only the suspicions of the parent, invariably the mother, that cracks the girl's denial.

The parents' initial negative reactions may, in fact, be what the girls were afraid of—disappointment, anger, and sadness. However, despite their dismay, all the parents I have met love their daughters fiercely, believe in them and in their potential, and want to do everything they can to help. Their primary concern is not the unborn child, but rather, *their* child.

In one of my first conversations with a mother while I was still working in Kansas, she told me that she had confided to her best friend that her daughter was pregnant and, because this was what the girl wanted, was taking her to have an abortion. The friend immediately brought up adoption as an alternative, and the mother asked in a voice filled with pain: "But what about *my* daughter?" I understood this to mean that this mother's main concern was not the baby, but her daughter, and what would be best for her.

I heard the same response from a young fetal-indication couple. The woman was especially afraid to tell her mother that she was having an abortion; her mother was so looking forward to her first grandchild. Finally, after the delivery, she called her mother to break the news. Her mother wondered why she hadn't told her earlier. My patient told her that she was afraid of disappointing her, to which her mother responded, "But you are my daughter. It's *you* that I care about."

Once I met a teenager who was an avid basketball player, hoping to get a basketball scholarship for college. I spent time with her mother, a gruff-appearing woman who poured her heart out to me, composed herself, then reverted to her gruff demeanor. She said that she rationalized her daughter's bodily changes, telling herself that her daughter's body was becoming like her father's, an ex-athlete. She described what happened after she finally found out the truth. "My husband and I sat in synagogue thinking that we're the type of people others talk about. How could we be so stupid and not know?" She said she felt morally torn about a later abortion after seeing the ultrasound, yet she had no doubt that her daughter's life was paramount. "I was afraid I'd find my daughter hanging in a closet." That is what mattered to her, that *her* child was alive. All else was secondary and paled in comparison.

At times, parents' resolve to help their daughter was rooted in family history. They learned from the past and were determined to prevent those mistakes from being repeated at their daughter's expense. One father brought in his daughter whose pregnancy was the result of rape, after she'd being given the date rape drug Rohypnol. He explained to me that he was motivated not just by his daughter's dire need but also by the story of his mother's birth. She had been a product of rape between *her* mother, a very young teenager, and a soldier staying at her parents' house during World War II. His mother grew up feeling unwanted and unloved, and those feelings never left her. Knowing the effects on mother and child, this father did not want his daughter to raise a child that she rejected, that she could not embrace and love wholeheartedly. He listened to her pleas for help to access an abortion and brought her to the clinic.

Another teen's family history also affected her parents' strong desire to help her have an abortion. She was accompanied by both her parents. Initially, she appeared depressed and withdrawn and, as is typical with maternal-indication patients, became a different person, beautiful and radiant, once she was no longer pregnant.

After her delivery, her relieved father, Lewis, tearfully told me: "In my family, we've had it the other way." When his sister was sixteen (she was now in her late forties) she got pregnant. As was the custom at the time, her parents sent her off in shame to a home for unwed mothers in a different town. After the birth, given no other option and under pressure from her parents, she relinquished the baby for adoption. Lewis remembered visiting her at the maternity home with their parents and how awkward and uncomfortable it was for everyone. He remembered her returning home a different person: She was once vibrant; now she was forlorn. She never talked about her experience and never had more children. She has suffered from severe depression ever since.

This history explained why, when Lewis and his wife found out that their daughter was pregnant, they went with her to talk to his parents. His parents told Lewis and his wife to do what was best, to do what *she* wanted, and that they had no judgment. They were living with regret for the decision they had made for their daughter over thirty years ago. And this is why Lewis felt so strongly the urgency to help his daughter. He said with great passion, "If I had to walk to Kansas, I would bring her here," and I believed him.

After my conversation with Kareem, I start caring for the day's first- and second-trimester patients. Intermittently, I check in on gurney to see how Amrita, Laura, and Jamie are doing. Amrita is in labor. She is bouncing on a large orange birthing ball between contractions and hunching over her gurney bed during the contractions. Arun is sitting beside her while her doula is sitting behind her, murmuring encouragement and applying pressure to her lower back with contractions, just as she had requested. Laura is lying quietly in bed, a counselor at her side. Despite her silence, I can tell that she's in labor by the tight grimaces that she makes every few minutes and how forcefully she holds the counselor's hand in those moments. Shortly afterward, she delivers without any complications, as does Amrita.

By the afternoon, Jamie is still not in labor. She looks tired and appears discouraged. We talk about pausing the induction until the next day, just as we had discussed in the group. Her cervix is ready, but the mysterious and unknowable switch that starts labor has not turned on yet. She is amenable to going back to the hotel, eating, getting some rest, and returning on Thursday. I remind her to call us if anything changes before then or if she goes into labor. The phone counselor will check in with her in the evening, and she should feel free to call if she has any questions or concerns. If she doesn't go into labor overnight, I'll see her Thursday morning, when we'll restart the induction.

It's possible that she'll go into labor during the night. Some patients just need to leave the clinic for labor to start. I remember one patient who did not have a single contraction all day. My plan was for her to return to her hotel and restart the induction the next day. She got dressed, went out to meet her mother in the waiting room, and right then went into labor. She walked back to gurney and immediately delivered. A more common scenario is for the patient to go back to the hotel, eat, sleep, and wake up in labor. What makes the difference? Is it the change of environment? The ability to relax in the hotel? Seeing the reassuring face of parents or partner? There is something about the onset of labor that is still not understood.

It's after 6:00 p.m. I have finished caring for the first- and second-trimester patients. Laura left the recovery room hours ago, looking tired but lighter. Once again, I eat trail mix for dinner, stream a mystery, and go to sleep. I have the feeling that I'll be busy tonight.

CHAPTER 8

The Death of Dr. George R. Tiller: May 31, 2009

Make no mistake, this battle is about
self-determination by women of the direction
and course of their family's lives.

—GEORGE R. TILLER, MD

It was 9:00 a.m. on Sunday, May 31, 2009, when the phone rang. I had flown home the evening before from my week of work at the Wichita clinic. I was happy. Even without George, who had spent the week at Disney World with his family, the week had gone well. My wife, Julie, and I were planning to celebrate our twenty-first anniversary.

I didn't recognize the caller's voice. She told me to sit down. "Who is this?"

"It's Cathy. Dr. Tiller has been shot and isn't with us."

George had been shot, and killed, by an anti-abortion zealot in his church, where he served as an usher. The saving grace was that he was killed instantly and did not suffer.

Julie and I began to weep. I ran from room to room, sobbing, crying, repeating, "This isn't right. This isn't right. This is *not* okay. This isn't what you do to someone because you don't like his job."

Eventually, I dropped down to the floor, wailed, and didn't stop for a long time.

This was the man I had hugged so many times, told so many times how much I appreciated him, how wonderful he was. Once,

I remember asking him, "Are you listening, do you hear what I'm saying? I want you to hear this. I want you to hear how wonderful you are." I can only hope that he did.

I caught the next flight back to Wichita, sobbing quietly in my window seat. As I was getting off the plane in Denver, the passenger who had been sitting next to me said gently, "I'm sorry that you have such a hard time flying." Amidst my grief, I had to smile. By then, I had been on that flight hundreds of times and fear of flying was extremely low on the list of things I worried about.

I responded, "It's not that. I just lost a good friend."

I was met right off the plane by federal marshals, who took me to a private waiting area and stayed with me until my connecting flight to Wichita took off. The murderer was still on the loose and wouldn't be caught until later that night. Were all third-trimester abortion providers going to be targeted that day, or was George the only one? It was still uncertain.

The next day, I went to see George's wife, Jeanne. She told me she was going to close the clinic, and I understood completely. The moment she had dreaded for years, maybe since the prior attempt on his life in 1993, had finally arrived. Her husband had sacrificed his life, and it was now time for others to carry on the work. She and her family had suffered enough.

The funeral was held a few days later. The church was filled with colleagues and friends. Julie, who had flown in, sat next to me and we were surrounded by the marshals. I was under their protection for several weeks after George's death, even while at home in Oakland. During the day, two of them sat outside on my porch and followed me everywhere, including to the swimming pool, where they sat on the bleachers. Ironically, their presence made me feel less secure, not more, because it meant I had something to be concerned about.

Years later, NoahLani recalled that time when he was thirteen years old and I was under federal marshal protection. He told me he stayed awake for three nights in a row, holding an assortment of kitchen knives, waiting to defend me should any additional anti-abortion murderers be inspired to act. He regularly watched the marshals circle the perimeter of the house with their flashlights and, in contrast to me, felt reassured by their presence.

One night, one of the marshals asked me, "Is there anything I can do for you?"

I replied, "Yes, you can bring back Dr. Tiller." Unfortunately, that wish was beyond his powers. Dr. Tiller could not be resurrected. After seven years, I had lost my home.

George's death was emotionally shattering for me. I realized everything I had told patients about grief now applied to me. At first, there was disbelief. In all our years together, I never thought he would be killed. I was sure that the era of killing abortion doctors had ended, that the tactics to stop abortions had moved on to the legislative front, enacting one restriction after another. It would be death by a thousand cuts, not by a bullet to the head.

George's death felt like the loss of my second father, and I grieved deeply. Three months before I met George, my father had died. We had grown very close in the years before his death, and I was still in mourning when I met George. There were few similarities between them. My father was on the short side, swarthy, and spoke with a thick Eastern European accent. His moral compass was somewhat askew, but his love for his family was without question. George, on the other hand, was tall and upright in posture and morals. He was guided equally by his love for his wife and four children and for justice. He was an honorable man.

Both my father and George, however, were without illusions and savvy about the ways of the world. My father would often say to me, "Shelley, it's a bullshit world." I taught George the expression, complete with the accent. He appreciated the sentiment and would repeat it, although he couldn't quite pull off the accent.

In the months after George's death, I kept a regular appointment with a friend who was a masseuse. Each time I entered her room, she lit candles. I sat, cried, and talked about George. She listened patiently and eventually gave me a soothing massage. But by October, after almost six months of this routine, I realized that

I was still an emotional mess. I started therapy. That, and time, did not heal the wounds, but it made them much more bearable.

George was dead. Women's Health Care Services was closed. I was in shock and in mourning, but I was determined to continue to provide third-trimester abortions. This was the work that meant so much to George, the cause he had given his life for. However, I didn't know what the next step should be. It was time, as George would have put it, "to paddle my own canoe."

The clinic closed the day after Dr. Tiller's assassination, and suddenly, we were all unemployed. For the staff, their work at the clinic was their career, and it was now over. WHCS was the only abortion clinic in Wichita. There was nowhere else where they could practice their specialized skills. Rather than look for new jobs, Cathy, the head nurse, and JoAn, the clinic director, decided to retire. JoAn never got the motorcycle Dr. Tiller had promised her if she worked until she was seventy-two. And after all the years that Cathy stood by and worked with Dr. Tiller, she, too, was ready to stop. The rest of the staff, a cohesive group that had withstood so many attacks over the years, disbanded, each looking for work wherever they could find it.

The three remaining doctors at Women's Health Care Services—Lee Carhart, Susan Robinson, and I—started looking for new homes. None of us faltered in our decision to continue the work, in whatever form it took. After George's death, Dr. Carhart struck out on his own, eventually opening a clinic in Maryland. Meanwhile, Dr. Susan Robinson and I developed a two-pronged approach in our search for work. Separately, we looked for work around the country and beyond—I even visited a clinic in Canada, where I could provide first- and second-trimester abortion care. But we were deeply committed to providing third-trimester abortion care and we hoped to find a clinic where we could practice together. We recognized the importance of continuing the work given that now there was only one other clinic in the entire country providing third-trimester abortions.

Susan was, like me, a California ob-gyn. We first met in the Bay Area, where we were both practicing in the 1990s. In 2005, three years after I started working with George, she also joined his practice. Before George's death, I rarely saw or spoke with Dr. Robinson; we each worked in Kansas when the other wasn't there, alternating our weeks of practice.

After George's death, however, Susan and I became inextricably linked. We became close colleagues and would eventually become known as a singular entity, "SusanAndShelley."

Initially, Susan reached out to Dr. Curtis Boyd and Dr. Glenna Halvorson-Boyd, longtime friends of George's, for possible employment providing first- and second-trimester abortion care at their clinic in Albuquerque, New Mexico. Curtis Boyd was one of the pioneers and innovators in the field of abortion care and was one of the doctors who trained George when he was first learning to perform second-trimester abortions. Dr. Boyd had provided safe, though *illegal*, abortions in Texas prior to *Roe*, and he was one of the first generation of doctors who provided care after the legalization of abortion in 1973. Glenna Halvorson-Boyd was a doctor of psychology who was instrumental in introducing and advancing counseling into the practice of abortion care. Curtis and Glenna were a complementary pair. Curtis worked with the medical staff; Glenna worked with the counseling staff.

I had heard about Curtis and Glenna for years before we formally met, and I regularly saw them together at the annual National Abortion Federation (NAF) meetings. As they made their entrance together into the conference room—Curtis with his impeccably groomed hair and well-cut suits and Glenna, stylishly dressed, with impossibly excellent posture—they seemed like abortion care royalty. Their sense of style was quite a contrast to the Kansas crew I was with, who dressed in a more down-home and comfortable style.

The Boyds owned and operated two clinics. They spent most of their time at their clinic in Dallas, Texas—Southwestern Women's Surgery Center—which provided abortions up to the legal gestational limit in Texas, which at that time was 21.6 weeks. This was a large, high-volume clinic, providing excellent care while complying with ever-increasing anti-abortion legislation. (The clinic was forced to close in early 2023, following the *Dobbs* decision overturning *Roe*.)

The Boyds' second clinic, Southwestern Women's Options (SWO), was in Albuquerque, New Mexico. It provided first- and second-trimester abortions and was a much smaller and lower-volume operation than the Dallas clinic. Both clinics were known throughout the country for their high level of care and their emphasis on counseling.

The Boyds were acutely aware of the void in third-trimester abortion care following Dr. Tiller's death. After Susan's overture, they decided to take things a step further and expand their practice to the third trimester. They invited "SusanAndShelley" to visit the Albuquerque clinic.

The difference between Southwestern Women's Options in Albuquerque and Women's Health Care Services in Wichita was startling. Due to constant threats of violence, WHCS was like a bunker. There was a guard at the entrance and a metal detector patients had to pass through. The few windows were small and offered minimal sunlight. In contrast, at SWO, there was no guard or metal detector, and the waiting room was bright, sunny, airy, and green, with large plants that were lovingly tended to. It immediately put me at ease and reminded me of Eve Surgical Center in LA, with its curved pathways and slideshow of changing seasons.

Nevertheless, it wasn't immune from the realities of abortion care in the United States. There were still protestors outside, although there were no sickle wielders in Albuquerque. As was par for the course for many abortion clinics, there had been at least one serious attack of violence at SWO. In 2007, the clinic, then at another location, was burned down by a patient's irate boyfriend. But since then, the clinic had reopened in this new building.

When we arrived, Susan and I were introduced to the SWO staff at their monthly clinic staff meeting, led by Abby, the clinic director. I noted that the staff felt comfortable discussing and processing their feelings about challenging situations that had arisen. They appeared to be a kind and thoughtful group. It felt good to be in that warm and caring environment, and after the trauma of George's death, it was a relief.

During a break in the meeting, I cornered Susan in a hall. I hadn't known what to expect, and I had already considered several options that didn't match what I was looking for. But here at SWO, I giddily proclaimed to Susan, "I'm in love." She, too, was excited to find such a compatible clinic.

That night, we had dinner with the Boyds, along with a doctor employed at the clinic who performed early abortions. She told me that Dr. Boyd loved dessert and, in the past, liked to order it for everyone as a first course. I also love dessert, which was obvious from my stint at the pastry shop, and this story about Curtis seemed like a good sign.

Susan and I wanted to continue to provide third-trimester abortion care; the Boyds wanted to offer that service; and the four of us seemed temperamentally suited. It was a good fit, and we agreed to work together. Susan and I were hired, and we began providing third-trimester abortion care in Albuquerque in January 2010, seven months after George's death.

CHAPTER 9

Thursday

I dread returning home, to the place where we had
planned to raise this baby. We had done so much
work to the house and had prepared the nursery.
My home will feel as empty as my heart.

—ANONYMOUS PATIENT

At 2:00 a.m. the phone rings. It's Margaret, the on-call phone counselor. She's the staff person who routinely calls third-trimester patients in the evening to check on them. She's also who patients call in the middle of the night when they think they might be in labor. Sometimes, patients just need reassurance. Sometimes, they are in very early labor, too early to come in. If that is the case, Margaret advises them to take a prescribed pain pill, go to bed, and call back in an hour if they are still awake. Often, patients fall asleep and Margaret doesn't hear back. Other times, it is clear the patient is in active labor and needs to come to the clinic.

Margaret tells me that she just spoke with Jamie. Twelve hours after being sent back to the hotel, she began feeling strong contractions. Robert is bringing her in.

Along with Delia and Skye, the on-call counselors, I meet the couple as they drive up to the clinic gate, which I unlock. I help Jamie out of the car, and there is no doubt that she is now in active labor. After an exam, during which I can feel how much her cervix has changed since the day before, we take her to gurney. Robert doesn't leave her side. Jamie is focused; staring at a fixed point between contractions and groaning loudly. Robert is nervous, talking quickly, telling Jamie how much he loves her. She quickly delivers with Robert at her side. They are both sobbing and hugging each other after the birth. After the D&C, she goes to the recovery room. They leave at 5:00 a.m., with the plan to return in the afternoon for the checkout exam. They told me earlier that they will not want to view the baby. They intend to work with a local funeral home to have the body shipped to a funeral home in their hometown and have a ceremony at their church.

The official day will start at 7:00 a.m. I'm tired. I decide it is more worthwhile to lie down and try to get some rest than to go swimming. Sometimes I feel too old to still be on call, to see patients during the day, to be up all night, and to work the next day.

We are available to patients twenty-four hours a day. If they have a problem in the middle of the night, they are advised to call us. If they need to be seen in the middle of the night, we will see them. In this practice, there is complete continuity, rather than fragmentation of care. This is the kind of medical care I believe in, I remind myself, as I get ready to face the new day.

The first patient of the day is Noor. Noor is very grumpy, as only a teenager can be. She's complaining of cramping, not strong enough for her to come into the clinic before her scheduled morning appointment, but enough to keep her up most of the night. I remove the laminaria and check her cervix. "Noor, I'm sorry that you couldn't sleep," I tell her. "But it was a *good* thing because your cervix did some really good work last night." Her cervix is soft, short, and starting to dilate. I anticipate a quick delivery, but I have learned the hard way not to share my positive predictions with patients. The one time I told a patient I thought she would deliver imminently, it took her *hours* to deliver. Far better to be encouraging without being specific. I have Noor go to gurney to be attended by her doula.

I see Irene next. From the outset, she has exhibited an incredible amount of equanimity and calm, which she maintains today. I imagine that these admirable qualities have enabled her to cope with her many challenges over the years—with single parenthood, financial insecurity, and now, with a recurrence of cancer in addition to this unintended pregnancy. I'm surprised to feel that her cervix is quite dilated and think that she *probably* will deliver quickly. But I again keep that thought to myself; I don't want to jinx her. I wonder who will deliver first, Irene or Noor. Meanwhile, I have patients waiting for their checkout exams.

LAURA AND AMRITA

Thursday marks the end of the abortion process for Laura, Amrita, Mary, and Jamie. The checkout exams are the culmination of the week for the third-trimester patients. It's a time for me to assess how they are doing before travelling home and for them to process the intense experience they have just come through. Seeing patients for the checkout exam offers them closure. They are done with the procedure; they can resume their lives, they can follow their dreams and aspirations, they can grieve. But the checkouts also provide closure for me.

Each week, I know that the person I meet on Tuesday morning—scared, anxious, angry, withdrawn—will not be the same person I see at the end of the week, a shift that Laura exemplifies.

When I enter Laura's room, I see a new woman. The air of heaviness and misfortune that weighed her down has lifted. Her defeated demeanor is gone, along with the pregnancy.

First, I attend to her physical exam. Her vital signs—temperature, blood pressure, and pulse—are all normal. She's having a minimal amount of bleeding and had only mild cramping overnight. She has been able to eat and sleep well for the first time in days. Before we begin our conversation, I have her lie on the exam table to check her belly and feel a firm uterus, a sign that it is contracting well and not bleeding excessively. It is also not tender, which is reassuring, as tenderness can be a sign of an infection. I have her sit back down on the chair and we chat.

A counselor has already gone over discharge instructions and precautions, and I answer her questions. She has been given a medication to prevent her breast milk from coming in so the distress and discomfort of lactation have been eliminated. While on the drive home, she knows to stop every two hours and walk around. This is to prevent blood clots from forming in her legs and lungs, an increased risk for women while pregnant and in the first weeks postpartum. She knows to call her doctor if she has increased bleeding, belly pain stronger than mild cramping, or a fever. And of course, she can always call us with any questions or concerns. She is to follow up with her doctor within a week.

I tell her, "There were no complications. Nothing that happened here will affect your ability to get pregnant, carry a pregnancy, or give birth." I'm not sure whether this matters for Laura, given the four children she has at home. But I want her to have the peace of mind, in case her hopes and goals ever change.

I ask her how she is feeling, and she is almost buoyant. She reports no complaints, no pain. And then she tells me something bigger—that she finally feels ready to leave her husband. I don't know whether this will happen; I cannot predict the future. But I know her future looks brighter and that she feels a renewed sense of possibility now that she is not burdened with another child.

After wrapping up with Laura, I see Amrita for her checkout exam. With her, there is no sense of buoyancy. I see a complex mix of sorrow and relief on her face. I'm not surprised. In general, for fetal-indication patients like Amrita, the loss weighs more heavily than it does with maternal-indication patients like Laura.

After the exam and a short private conversation, we welcome Arun into the room. When I ask how they're feeling, they tell me they're sad. But they are also sure they made the right decision. Since the delivery, they have been focused on the hugs and kisses they will give to and receive from their two-year-old when they arrive home. They light up when they talk of their girl, who has been lovingly cared for by Amrita's mother while the couple is in Albuquerque. I ask if they can show me a photo, and I see a beaming, smiling little girl. I'm glad she'll be there to greet them.

Amrita and Arun tell me they have arranged cremation as they'd hoped, and they are going to scatter the ashes when they return to India to visit their families. On the baby's due date, they are planning to mark the occasion by supporting a child in an orphanage in India. I am deeply moved by their generosity.

MARY

Mary is next, and of today's four checkouts, she is the only one who has chosen to view her baby. One of our counselors, Flora, is preparing the baby for the viewing, so the couple can spend as much time as they would like with their baby. Afterward, they have opted for cremation and will have the ashes shipped to them. While Flora works, I see Mary alone in a procedure room.

Physically, Mary is doing well. Now we move on to feelings. Mary tells me that she's both happy and sad: happy that she is done and sad that she is done. Her baby is no longer physically connected to her, and she feels a void. She believes this was the best decision she and Christopher could have made, but that doesn't take away the pain.

I can't take away that pain either. What I tell her is that the acute pain and sense of loss she's feeling right now will get better. The sharpness will ease. What will never go away is the love she has for her child. That love will always be with her.

Given her age, I'm not sure what her future plans for childbearing are, and at this point, she probably doesn't know either. I reassure her that there were no complications and no impediments to future conception.

When Flora has finished preparing for the viewing, it is time to bring Mary and Christopher into a counseling room. I tell them that their baby, who they named Gabriel, is beautiful, and then I describe the physical anomaly that I noticed, a very large defect in the baby's spine. I ask whether they are ready to see him, and they are. Before I leave the room, I light a candle.

I bring Gabriel in a basket and place him on a chair facing Mary. A blanket covers the basket. Mary looks at Christopher, who nods. Then, with quivering fingers, she removes the blanket. Both of them stare intently at Gabriel and both start crying. Mary hesitates, turns to me, and asks, "May I touch him?" I say yes, and she does. "May I pick him up?" I say yes, and she does. She picks up Gabriel in his blanket, holds him, and cradles him in her arms, looking at him lovingly in the way all new parents do. I ask if they want me to point out the defect and they demur. I then ask if they want me to step out to give them some privacy, and they do. Eventually, Christopher steps out to let me know they are done. I come in the room to take Gabriel away. In the room, I feel anguish, love, and intimacy. It feels like the room is vibrating with a sacred energy.

When I come back to the room, that feeling has dissipated. I see a sad but much softer couple than the one I met two days ago. Mary is no longer anxious. Christopher is no longer tense and suspicious. As the week progressed, I sensed that his attitude had changed, from hostile to open. "It's been quite an eye-opening experience," he tells me now, and I believe him. What strikes me the most, and what I will never forget, is the last thing he says before our goodbyes: "Quite frankly, my religion has let me down." Would that it were not so, I think to myself.

After their abortion, not infrequently, patients send us cards or flowers thanking us for their care. Mary and Christopher are a couple I never expected to hear from again. I imagined they would want to put this experience behind them and never think again about the time they went to an abortion clinic.

Years later, however, I saw another fetal-indication patient from the same state. She told me her genetic counselor had referred her to a patient who had been to the clinic in the past and who would be happy to talk about her experience. That was Mary.

NOOR AND IRENE

As soon as I escort Mary and Christopher out of the clinic, I hear "gurney transport" on the overhead page, the code that someone has delivered. One minute later, I hear it again! Both Noor and Irene have delivered, first Irene, then Noor.

I go to perform both D&Cs, starting with Irene. At the completion of the D&C, I go to the head of the table to let her know that she is all done and that everything has gone well. Calm, serene Irene bursts into convulsive sobs. When she catches her breath, she tells me how happy and relieved she is. Now she can resume her cancer treatment and continue to mother her teenage daughter. Now she can live. I leave the room teary-eyed and have to pull myself together as I walk to Noor's procedure room for the D&C.

Noor has done well. Her bleeding is normal and there are no complications. We are very busy and there are a lot of first- and second-trimester patients to be seen, but I take a moment to tell her father, Kareem, that she is done and there were no complications. A big smile breaks out on his face. Given what I had observed of their relationship on the first day, I tell Kareem that his daughter might not thank him now, but with time, she will see and appreciate how much he helped her. He listens and says, "Yes, we've [he and his wife] made mistakes too and only later realized how much our parents helped us." I love how he is now able to empathize with his daughter, while two days ago he struggled to understand her. I can only read so much into it, but it seems that their time in Albuquerque, as stressful as it was, has brought them closer together.

JAMIE

Throughout the rest of the day, I meet the other clinic patients, as I also have first- and second-trimester patients to care for. In the late afternoon, it comes time for Jamie's checkout exam and then my final meeting with her and Robert. My day starts and ends with Jamie, and I wonder which of us is more tired. She's doing well. Robert has been in touch with their pastor several times during their stay in Albuquerque, and the pastor continued to offer them his support, walking with them during this hard time in their lives.

As we part, I receive many hugs from the two of them. Then I have a question for them. I ask if it would be okay with them for me to contact their pastor, and if so, whether they could share his number. With their permission, I call the pastor and let him know how much I have appreciated his support and how much it meant to Jamie and Robert. He replies, "I wouldn't want to be in that situation. I wanted them to know they had our support." He said that he appreciated my call. I had just spoken to an evangelical Christian pastor, and he had just spoken warmly to an abortion provider. God works in mysterious ways.

All the third-trimester patients have delivered. Tomorrow I'll see Irene and Noor for their checkout exams. As the day ends, I'm exhausted, but I feel light.

New Mexico: 2000s

I honestly think you saved my life.

—ANONYMOUS PATIENT

When Susan and I were hired to work at SWO in 2010, it was an opportunity to create a third-trimester practice from the ground up. Curtis Boyd and Glenna Halvorson-Boyd gave us the backing and freedom to set up the practice as we envisioned it. They were rarely there, mainly working in their very busy Dallas clinic, and they had no experience with third-trimester abortion care, so they had no preconceived notions and gave us free rein. Abby, the clinic director, wholeheartedly supported our efforts to build a new and different practice.

Susan and I were able to take all we had learned from and appreciated about Women's Health Care Services and add additional features that we thought were important for good care. From Kansas, we brought many of George's instruments and the two birthing chairs and stools I had encouraged him to buy. Inspired by another clinic, Susan introduced the idea of placing notebooks beside every recliner in the patient recovery room for patients to write about their experiences and share their feelings. The next patient sitting in the recliner would be able to read earlier entries and feel supported.

More importantly, we brought Dr. Tiller's philosophy that stressed patients' emotional well-being and was concordant with the Boyds' approach. We liked how counseling was conducted at

SWO. It went well beyond the depth and care of standard abortion clinic counseling—and we wanted that to continue. But we also felt, based on our experience in Kansas, that group sessions were invaluable for the third-trimester patients. At the end of each week in Wichita, patients who had initially been wary of the group session often told me how helpful it had been, how much it had meant to talk with people who knew exactly what they were experiencing. Although this was a new concept for SWO, Abby was receptive to the idea of group sessions, and she incorporated them into the schedule.

Once Susan and I established our philosophy and approach, our immediate challenge was to integrate third-trimester care into an existing clinic that previously had only provided first- and second-trimester abortions. The clinic culture in Albuquerque was much more informal than in Wichita. Counselors wore neat street clothes rather than scrubs, and Dr. Boyd was "Curtis" to the staff.

The expansion of the practice to the third trimester was a big adjustment for the staff. They saw how third-trimester patients' needs were different. On the whole, the patients were more desperate than first- and second-trimester patients. Because of the travails of accessing the abortion, they were also more stressed when they arrived at the clinic. They required more time, more patience, and more attention. The practice and timing of third-trimester abortions was also very different. First- and second-trimester abortions are procedures that last minutes. In contrast, a third-trimester abortion is not a procedure; it's a process. It involves the patient going through labor, which, although it is shorter than a full-term delivery, usually lasts hours, not minutes. Third-trimester abortion requires intense care through labor and the subsequent intact delivery of a stillborn. It has more in common with midwifery and obstetrics than abortion care, which means it requires a different mindset and a different set of skills.

Not surprisingly, over time, much of the original counseling staff left, replaced by those who entered the practice knowing to expect third-trimester abortions and stillborn deliveries, in addition to first- and second-trimester procedures.

One of the new staff members was Reyna, a twenty-five-year-old first-generation Honduran American born and raised in New Mexico. She started working at the clinic as a medical assistant, counselor, and doula. After being raised Catholic and taught her whole life that abortion "no es cosa de Dios"—is not a thing of God—she changed her mind when her older sister needed an abortion after getting pregnant during an abusive relationship. "I remember my sister crying herself to sleep many nights," Reyna told me. But her devout family coerced her sister to continue the pregnancy. Reyna's sister's son was now sixteen years old and her sister adored him, but life had not been easy. Through this experience, both Reyna and her sister realized on a deep and personal level the importance of abortion as an option, and Reyna decided to make it the focus of her career. Listening to Reyna, I was reminded of JoAn, my colleague in Kansas. Both JoAn's and Reyna's sisters had been young and had unplanned pregnancies with abusive partners. In the 1960s, abortion was illegal, inaccessible to JoAn, and not talked about. Forty or so years later, abortion was legal and accessible to Reyna's sister, yet religious doctrine prevented her from obtaining one.

With the contribution of staff members like Reyna, Susan and I were able to utilize the best elements from our experiences and training to create a unique practice that resonated with our values. We started our practice in Albuquerque using the same medical protocols we had learned in Wichita, and over time, we made gradual adjustments based on our experience.

Although the medications used to induce labor in Wichita and Albuquerque were similar, our approach differed once labor began. In Wichita, patients labored in the large gurney room with curtains dividing the narrow gurney beds. They were medicated heavily under Dr. Tiller's variant of twilight sleep, an early twentieth-century technique used by ob-gyns for pain relief. Patients in Wichita were awake during contractions and asleep between them. This meant they were essentially in bed throughout their labor, attended by staff who administered medication under the doctor's supervision and assessed their well-being.

In Albuquerque, with the freedom to make changes, and with my background, I helped evolve the practice toward a midwifery model of care. Early on, we hired midwives to set the tone and implement this approach. The midwives trained the counselors, like Reyna, to become abortion doulas, labor attendants who were integral to patients' labor and delivery.

Each patient was assigned a doula who stayed with her throughout the day. The doula embodied the "power of presence," a foundation of the midwifery model, which holds that intervention is not always needed, but that a calm and steady presence offering comfort and reassurance is paramount. The doulas' compassionate presence helped relieve patients' anxiety. Lowering their stress level helped labor to progress and increased their ability to tolerate it.

Before we introduced this concept, the staff felt that they always had to be *doing* something. Instead, we reinforced the value of sitting with patients by their gurney beds even before the medication we administered to induce labor took effect, while they were still resting or asleep. When they woke up, they could look around and know someone was with them, that they were not alone, and they felt safe. The long hours they spent together led to deep connections between the patients and their doulas. Patients told me innumerable times how comforted they were by this approach. One patient said, "I felt supported the whole time. I felt like I had a family member with me at all times."

We held regular trainings in labor support. The first part was conducted by Tewa Women United, a Native woman–led, community-based organization committed to reproductive health and justice for Indigenous women. They taught the staff a historical and political context for labor support. The second part of the training, led by the clinic staff, included the nuts and bolts of labor and how to support the laboring patient, both physically and emotionally, using movement, massage, birthing balls, and birthing chairs. The two sessions complemented one another.

This model of care began as soon as the patient walked into gurney to start the induction. For many patients, this was their first experience of labor, and they were often anxious and afraid. The goal of the initial interaction with the gurney staff was to help patients feel secure and safe. The room was calm and peaceful, scented with lavender, with dimmed lights and soft music playing. The patient was introduced to her doula, who let her know the plan of the day, that medications would be given to induce labor, that her vital signs would be checked regularly, and that she could rest until the medications took effect. She was reassured that nothing would happen without her knowledge. The doula tucked her patient into the gurney bed, brought blankets, and offered drinks and snacks as needed. Once labor kicked in, the doula was right beside her to help her cope. Instead of going into twilight sleep, the patient was encouraged to move around and change positions as she pleased. Pain medication was administered judiciously.

Helping patients cope in labor involved many different modalities that often changed as the labor progressed. Relaxation techniques were essential to handle the intensity of contractions. Some patients focused on their doula, making eye contact and breathing in unison. Some focused on a movement such as rocking back and forth on the birthing ball. Some patients were comforted by heat on their lower backs; some preferred ice. Some found comfort in massage or just pressure on their back. The doula keyed into what helped the individual patient and always asked permission before initiating any touch. The doulas recognized that many of our patients had a history of trauma, either related to their pregnancy or in their past, and it was important for patients to have as much control over their bodies as possible.

Language and tone were also important components of care. Recognizing how sensitive patients are in labor, doulas spoke in soft, calm voices. They reassured and encouraged their patients who could get discouraged in the throes of labor and said things like

"I'm trying, but I can't do this. I can't. I can't." Doulas responded with, "Yes, I can see how hard you are trying. You are doing well. You got this. You are so strong. You can do this."

In this setting, there were moments of beauty, tenderness, and joy—and, in the case of a very wanted baby, moments of intense grief. The ability to create an atmosphere conducive to peaceful births, whether in grief or in joy, was one of the things that made this work so rewarding.

Maya, a teenage patient, delivered rapidly in the squatting position. Before each big push, she spontaneously counted out loud, "One, two, three," and when the baby came out, she yelled, "I did it all by myself. It's out. I'm so happy." When her mother came into the room after delivery, she exclaimed, "Mommy, I did it!"

I attended a very different delivery with my mentee, Kalin. A licensed midwife, she was a former counselor at the clinic who returned as a medical student for a reproductive health rotation. Together we attended Audrey in labor.

Audrey was a fetal-indication patient with a highly treasured pregnancy. Given the baby's severe anomaly, she and her husband, Mark, had decided that the most loving thing they could do as parents was to let their child go.

To distract herself in labor, Audrey read a trashy novel, holding the book in her hand between contractions. Eventually, as her contractions got stronger, I asked her if it was okay for us to take the book from her hand. She agreed, and Kalin marked the spot. Audrey quickly felt the urge to push, and she rapidly pushed out her baby, Elijah.

She had told us beforehand that she wanted to hold her baby right after delivery, rather than wait until the next day, as was most commonly done. We put Elijah on her chest and she held him, skin to skin. It was beautiful, moving, and heartbreaking to be with her, listening to her cooing, watching her gaze intently at her child, as I imagine she had done after the births of her other children. This was during the Covid pandemic, and partners were not allowed in the room. With her permission, we put Mark on FaceTime, and the two parents spent hours together with their baby.

Practicing in New Mexico was a stark contrast to practicing in Kansas. In Wichita, the atmosphere within the clinic walls had always been peaceful, supportive, and compassionate. But outside it was pure rancor. It wasn't just the crowds of protestors and the Trash Truck. The legal and political environment for abortion care in Kansas was hostile. New Mexico was much more hospitable, and the difference in the legal landscape was apparent as soon as we started to see patients at SWO. The difference reshaped our care and how we approached patients in the third trimester, and it soon reshaped my overall thinking about abortion care.

In Kansas, years of ever-tightening restrictions meant that patients seeking a third-trimester abortion had to go through a strict screening process. At the time when Dr. Tiller and I practiced in Kansas, post-viable abortions, defined by the legislature as those performed at twenty-four weeks or later, were banned *except* to preserve the life or health of the mother. A subsequent Kansas Supreme Court had clarified that "preserve the life or health" also included the mental health of the mother. (However, following Dr. Tiller's death, legislation passed allowing post-viable abortions only in cases of substantial and/or irreversible *physical* harm.) To meet these requirements, Kansas law mandated that the treating physician and a second Kansas physician, unaffiliated with the clinic, both agree and attest to the fact that continuing the pregnancy would cause substantial and/or irreversible physical and/or mental harm to the mother.

For any woman who wanted to qualify for an abortion in Kansas, it was an ordeal. She had to convince at least two doctors that continuing the pregnancy would cause substantial or irreversible harm to her. Essentially, she had to tell a story that was compelling enough to prove that she "deserved" to have an abortion.

At Dr. Tiller's clinic, there was a screening process in place to ensure that our patients met these requirements. It started with an interview over the phone with a counselor who sought to determine whether the patient qualified under Kansas law. The counselor started with a series of questions: How long have you known that you are pregnant? Why do you not want to be pregnant? Have you considered adoption? What would be the consequences if you could not get an abortion? Have you had any thoughts about trying to cause a miscarriage?

Then the counselor would ask a second series of questions about whether the patient was at a health risk or whether they exhibited signs of a major depressive disorder or other psychiatric disturbances—for example, suicidal thoughts or attempts—that might lead to substantial or irreversible harm to her. The counselor also needed to ask important questions relating to the prospective patient's medical and surgical history to ascertain whether the woman could be safely cared for in the outpatient setting. If they were at *too* much of a health risk, they could not be seen at the clinic.

After the full panel of questions, the counselor would bring the intake information to the doctor for a careful review. If the doctor thought the patient qualified under Kansas law, the prospective patient was invited to be seen, with the proviso that there would be further evaluation once she came to the clinic. At this stage, there were always patients who could not be accepted, either because they did not qualify or because they were deemed too high-risk to be cared for at the clinic. For those who passed the initial screening and came to the clinic, the treating physician working at the clinic that week evaluated the patient further, followed by the second unaffiliated Kansas physician. It was only after all these evaluations that the patient could be approved for third-trimester care.

In New Mexico, by contrast, there were no legal restrictions on post-viable abortions, nor a requirement for a second physician to approve the abortion. I did not realize, initially, how much this would change my approach.

In New Mexico, we still employed phone counselors as the first point of contact with potential patients. However, rather than intensively screen callers to see if they met all the qualifications required by law, the phone counselors in New Mexico could focus on *counseling*, gathering information while providing reassurance and support. Phone counselors used a similar template of questions as in Kansas, but they used these as a starting point to gain a better understanding of the patients' situations, to supply them with information about the abortion process, and to address their fears and concerns. Initial conversations usually lasted forty-five minutes to an hour and were the first of multiple conversations, as counselors continued to work with the same prospective patient to help her with financial and logistical arrangements and answer the many questions that arose.

When I first came to Albuquerque, I used the phone intake as I did in Kansas. It began with my evaluation of prospective patients, serving as the first step in the arduous process of qualification. I was used to reading the intakes to see if patients met certain criteria, but I soon realized I was perpetuating the notion that only some situations or conditions were "deserving" of an abortion, a notion that persists today in discussions of exceptions to abortion bans.

Instead, I found that I could approach each case quite differently in Albuquerque. I still reviewed each intake to learn about patients' life circumstances. But they no longer needed to convince me that they were "worthy" of an abortion. In a state with no gestational limits, I was now able to listen to each woman fully, without trying to diagnose her, without having to fit her into a slot that allowed her to qualify for an abortion. It felt liberating to be in a setting where a state legislature was not dictating lifesaving healthcare.

I was able to spend so much more time really listening to the women I cared for in New Mexico because I wasn't legally bound to assign them a psychiatric disorder to explain their decision to end their pregnancies. I still wasn't able to accept everyone as a patient, of course. I still needed to turn away patients I considered too high-risk to be cared for in the outpatient setting, but I could let my decision-making process be focused on the individual woman in front of me, on her situation, on her story. I already knew that no one takes a third-trimester abortion lightly; the fact that so many women were willing to overcome so many barriers to access one had shown me that for years.

As I reviewed the phone intakes, what struck me most was the despair of the women seeking third-trimester care. It was heartbreaking and, at times, breathtaking. These women knew our clinic was one of the few in the country that could help them, and if we were unable to care for them, they would be forced to continue their pregnancies. A twenty-five-year-old said, "It is so hard to live right now. I don't hug anyone or stand in front of them too long for fear of somebody finding out. I just need help because I am afraid for my life. If this continues, I will end my life. I'm just trying to hold on a little longer. I am trapped in this body. There is no way out."

Another patient said, "The belief that I always had that I could somehow handle everything that God faced me with gave me a sense of strength. I don't see how I could go on living if I were not able to have an abortion. I feel so worn down by this whole ordeal [trying to get an abortion for the last two months]. I never understood how people could ever get to the point that they could just give up on their life and want it all to go away. I understand how life can push a person to that point now. I know how it feels to just want everything to go away. I used to love my life. It scares me so much that I could even consider giving up. I never thought I could feel so desperate. I want so badly to feel happy again. I want to enjoy my family and friends and my life the way I used to."

This woman expressed what so many others felt. They were surprised by the strength of their feelings, and they *never* imagined that they would feel this way. Given the distress of the women I saw, I was often relieved that in New Mexico there were no arbitrary gestational age cutoffs or very limited exceptions to these cutoffs, as there are in many states. So often, rape and incest are the exceptions to abortion restrictions. But the more patients I saw, the more I listened to them tell me their stories and circumstances, the more I wondered, *why?* Are these the two worst things that could ever befall anyone? Do you have to be a rape or incest survivor to be given the "privilege" of having an abortion? I heard too many women tell me about their intolerable situations to continue to believe in a hierarchy of desperation.

I also heard enough stories to learn that how women feel about their pregnancies is as important, if not more so, than the external realities of their lives. What might be tolerable for one person might be completely intolerable for someone else. And there isn't an objective, easily definable cutoff that determines when desperation sets in. Instead, what became clear to me is that when desperation does strike, it drives women to take whatever measures are necessary.

All the free diapers and formula offered by protestors outside abortion clinics are meaningless to someone who is determined to end a pregnancy. A patient told the phone counselor, "I just don't know where I would go or what to do if I couldn't have the abortion. I feel like I'm trapped in a nightmare and won't wake up. I never knew that I could be such a lifeless person with such monstrous thoughts, and it hurts to know that I'm that person because of a baby."

For many women, having an abortion is their salvation. As a mother of three who was living in a shelter for battered women and deathly afraid of her husband said, "Having this abortion unfortunately is my sanity," *and,* "Not having this abortion would be like signing my own death certificate."

The absolute necessity and lifesaving nature of third-trimester abortion care was clear to me from my time in Kansas. But there, legal constraints shaped how we approached care. Freed from these constraints in New Mexico, we were able to focus solely on patient care, as it should be in all healthcare settings.

The political landscape was also very different. When Susan and I first arrived in Albuquerque in 2010, the state house of representatives, senate, and governorship, under Bill Richardson, were all

Democratic. After his term expired due to term limits, he was succeeded by an anti-abortion Republican, Susana Martinez, the first female and first Latina to be elected as governor of New Mexico. She served from 2011–2019. She was no friend of the clinic, but the Democratic legislature was able to keep her in check. The political situation in New Mexico was the opposite of Kansas, a notably red state, where the legislature was overwhelmingly Republican with a Democratic governor, Kathleen Sebelius, who served from 2003–2009.[1]

Despite the fact that the Democrats controlled the legislature in New Mexico, there were still political challenges, especially once our third-trimester practice opened. Every legislative session, pro-choice groups lobbied hard to maintain existing protections for abortion care and block encroachment. These groups arose from a community that, for the most part, openly supported abortion care. The days of supportive comments whispered sotto voce by people in Wichita were behind me. I felt welcomed in Albuquerque; I was no longer working in the shadows. I felt liberated after the intense, never-ending attacks and harassment in Kansas.

But still, I never stopped missing Dr. Tiller. Sometimes a patient would come into the clinic in the middle of the night with a challenging dilemma, and in these moments I would often think of Dr. Tiller and try to channel his wisdom.

One day, in our last year together, Dr. Tiller turned to me and said, "You are my gift to the next generation." Creating the third-trimester abortion practice in Albuquerque allowed me to put the remarkable gifts he gave me to good use. In collaboration with a dedicated staff, incorporating best medical and counseling practices and instituting a midwifery model of care, an extraordinary clinic rose from the despair following George's death. I know he would be proud.

CHAPTER 11

Friday

Oh my god! I look in the mirror
and see me again.

—ANONYMOUS PATIENT

The alarm goes off at 5:00 a.m. The work week is almost over. I
have a lot less energy than I had on Tuesday, but I force myself
to go to my 5:30 a.m. workout, knowing I have never regretted a
morning swim. I arrive at the clinic, and before seeing patients,
I begin to write follow-up letters to all the clinics, genetic counselors, and doctors who have referred this week's third-trimester
patients. Later in the day, I'll also call them or leave a message if
I can't reach them. These letters and calls let providers know how
the week went for their patients, and I also thank them for the
referral.

If I'm calling an abortion clinic that couldn't see a patient because she had passed their gestational limit, the staff are relieved
to know she received care. Typically they don't hear back from the
patients they had to turn away. They may have just talked to them
over the phone or met them only once. My call is the only way they
will know the patient has overcome all the barriers, jumped through
all the hoops, and received the safe care she so desperately needed.

The fetal-indication patients' providers are often sending their
patients not to the specialist across the hall but to the abortion
clinic outside their state. These providers care about their patients
and are often frustrated that they cannot care for them themselves.
Hearing that all has gone well is especially gratifying.

Just as patients are surprised by the level of care at our clinic— I've lost count of the number of times patients have told me that this is the best healthcare that they've ever received, which both satisfies and dismays me—so are providers who refer a patient for the first time. They are not expecting to get a phone call from the abortion provider, nor are they expecting to hear such positive reports from their returning patients.

Still, there are always exceptions. The doctor of a fetal-indication patient was sent a follow-up letter after he couldn't be reached by phone. In return, he sent a letter back sternly requesting never to be contacted again. From the tone of the letter, it was clear that he did not want to have anything to do with an abortion provider or an abortion clinic.

After I write a few letters, it comes time for the last two check-out exams, following up with Irene and Noor after their deliveries yesterday.

IRENE

When I enter Irene's room, I find that her serene and composed demeanor has returned. She appears pensive when I ask her how she's feeling. She says that she feels relieved. She has an appointment with her oncologist next week and will shortly begin treatment. Her dreams of attending nursing school and seeing her daughter through college now seem possible again. And yet . . .

She tells me she is aware of what she has done, that she has ended the potential life of her child. She is sad about that, but she believes she made the right decision. Under the current circumstances of her life—as a single mother living with financial insecurity, facing a recurrence of cancer requiring treatment—this is the course she needed to take. Perhaps, if her life were different, she would have made a different decision, but this is the life she has.

She asks me to thank all the staff members, who she names individually, for the care they provided. Her voice cracks when she answers one of the standard questions I ask: "Do you have any regrets?"

"No," she says. "You and your staff saved my life. Thank you." Before I walk her out of the clinic, she embraces me tightly. I can feel her gratitude, and I hope she can feel mine as well. I am grateful I was able to provide care that has been a lifeline for her. Just as with Laura, I cannot know what her future brings, but I hope her cancer treatment goes smoothly and that she and her daughter have many more years together.

NOOR

Noor is the last third-trimester patient I see this week. I walk into the room to see a radiant and bubbly teenager. What a difference from the unhappy young woman I met on Tuesday! She's excited to go back to college and restart her life. She tells me that she and her father have been talking more the last couple of days than they have in years. They even discussed birth control, which astonishes Noor, because she thought her parents would continue to expect her to be abstinent.

We meet alone first, and we talk about her relationship with her parents. I remind her that even though they may not approve of everything she does, they care about her and support her. This week has been strong proof of that. I hope she now knows that she can turn to her parents when she's in crisis, rather than try to shoulder the burden herself. After I say goodbye to Noor, I pop into the waiting room to say goodbye to Kareem, who has been waiting there for her. I wish them all my best. They both have done well this week.

It's during the checkout exams that I see the transformative power of abortion care, sometimes literally. In contrast to the drab baggy clothes maternal-indication patients wear on Tuesday to hide their pregnancies, by their checkout exams, they have replaced them with tight jeans, bright colored shirts, and makeup. There is an openness to their faces I hadn't seen before. Their personalities shine through, and they are glowing. It makes sense. They have been relieved of a huge physical and emotional burden, and it shows.

There are some, like Irene, who are more contemplative at the end of the week, and I am struck by the contrast between Irene and Noor. Irene's reaction is more similar to what I generally see in fetal-indication patients. They, too, emerge from the week looking different. Their clothes remain the same; after all, the pregnancy was not hidden. But they look more relaxed and at peace. They are still sad, just as they were at the beginning of the week, but the air of worry and anxiety is gone.

Always, when I meet with the patients on their last day, I ask them how they are feeling. It is a simple question, but the answers are anything but simple. The overwhelming feeling expressed by all my patients is one of relief, but it is a different kind of relief for the two groups and for each individual. The fetal-indication patients and their partners are relieved that they are safe, that they now can move forward from this great loss and continue their emotional healing process. They are mourning the loss of their child, who had been living inside them for so many months and is now gone. Like Mary, they might express feelings of emptiness. It is not a relief that they are no longer pregnant. It is a relief to know that they have spared their child a lifetime of suffering and hardship, which brings with it a sense of resoluteness. Despite all the pain they carry, they believe they did the right thing. They have gotten through the hardest part of their journey. They now have the confidence to get through the next.

In contrast, the maternal-indication patients are relieved that they are no longer pregnant. For those who have been trying to access an abortion for months, for those who are finally able to escape their abusive partners, for those who were raped, for those who are trying to finish middle school, high school, or college, the abortion lifts a tremendous burden that they have carried for months. They might express the sense of exultation that one teenager voiced: "I feel great. It's still too good to be true." Or they may have Irene's more reflective response, considering all the factors surrounding them, and how, in another world, things might have been different. I continually appreciate how patients like Irene are able to acknowledge these feelings yet still come to the determination that they are making the right choice for this particular pregnancy at this particular time. A patient spoke for many when she said, "Okay—so no one wants to be here, but we all make difficult choices sometimes that are for the best."

There is an old trope, commonly seen on anti-abortion posters, that says women regret their abortions. I always ask maternal-indication patients whether they feel any regret following the abortion. In response to this question, I've never heard a patient say that she regretted having the abortion. In contrast to the beginning of the week, when patients will often reveal that they're afraid they *might* feel regret, at the end of the week, it is extremely rare to hear any feelings of regret at all.

In my experience, if patients do express regret, it's regret for the circumstances that led them to seek an abortion.[1] Often women will regret that they didn't recognize the pregnancy earlier or that they weren't able to access an abortion sooner. A fourteen-year-old told me what she regretted: "Having sex. Birth control will be my first step when I get back home." A mother of four told me, "I hate that I had to do it, but it was the best decision for me and the children I already have. They're already here."

My patients—Irene and Noor, Mary and Jamie, Amrita and Laura—are doing the best they can. But they live in the real world, and they know that. They have no illusions about their circumstances and their capabilities.

Those feelings are expressed in the recovery room notebooks, in their full sense of love and sorrow and clarity. As one patient wrote: "The first time I heard your heartbeat melted my heart. It was the best feeling ever! Please forgive your Daddy and me for doing this. As much as I would love to take care of you, show you the world and be the best mommy—but you know, I am not ready to do that now. Physically, mentally, spiritually and financially. I am incapable of being a mother to you. Just know that you'll always be my first baby and I will never ever forget you. You will always be in your father and my heart, mind and soul. Forgive me for doing this to you. I will always love you, my precious angel. Lots of love, Mommy."

CHAPTER 12

Beyond Friday

Abortion is about women's
hopes, dreams, potential.

—GEORGE R. TILLER, MD

Do the feelings my patients express to me at the checkout exam change over time? I often wonder what happened to all the patients I cared for. If I hear back from patients, it's often right afterward, perhaps a gift of flowers, perhaps a thank-you card. But what about years later? Did Laura finally manage to leave her abusive husband? Did Irene's cancer go back in remission, and did she become a nurse anesthetist? Did Amrita have a second healthy child? And, years later, how did these patients integrate this profound experience into their lives?

Did this experience empower them to believe they can get through difficult times and do hard things? Did it leave them feeling that they had agency over their bodies and their lives? I usually don't know. I can only hope that this decision helped them live the lives they wanted and deserved. Rarely, patients have stayed in contact and I get a glimpse of their future lives.

ROSE

One of the first patients I cared for when I moved my practice to Albuquerque was Rose, a twenty-four-year-old living on the West Coast. Rose had struggled with alcoholism since she was sixteen and had been in and out of rehab for years, and on and off the streets. Pregnancy was the last thing she considered when she felt nauseated and bloated. She often felt that way. However, when Rose made a rare visit to her parents, her mother, noting her belly, strongly suspected pregnancy and took her to a local Planned Parenthood. The bloating was not due to her heavy drinking but to a twenty-six-week pregnancy.

Rose was certain that she needed an abortion. She was concerned both for herself and her child. And, given her heavy drinking, there was a high likelihood that this child would suffer from fetal alcohol syndrome, characterized by distinct facial features and intellectual and behavioral disabilities. She didn't think her child should suffer from her inability to stop drinking, and she didn't think she could handle caring for a child.

Rose and her mother flew to Albuquerque for a third-trimester abortion. All went well. At the checkout exam, she told me she felt that the abortion had given her a second chance. She was determined to restart her life. When I said goodbye, I could only hope that this was so.

Every Christmas, for over ten years, I received a holiday card from Rose. The abortion *had* been a turning point in her life. She had stopped drinking and had gotten her life together. She was doing well.

Rose was a maternal-indication patient. For her, ending the pregnancy was a chance to regain control of her life. What was it like for a fetal-indication patient, someone whose pregnancy was intentional and welcomed?

CARLY

It was December 2005 when Carly, her husband, and both sets of parents came to Women's Health Care Services in Wichita for an abortion.[1] She was twenty-seven weeks pregnant when her baby, Eli, was diagnosed with severe brain anomalies, despite prior normal ultrasounds. Ironically, at the time, she was working as a genetic counselor focused on prenatal diagnosis and counseling.

Carly and I stayed in touch for a few years after her abortion. One year, we ran into each other at a conference. By then, she had gone on to have two more children. After we hugged and sat down, I noticed she was wearing a bracelet with her first son's name, Eli, engraved on it. Eli was clearly still very present in her heart and thoughts.

Eighteen years after her abortion, while working on this book, I got back in touch with Carly, and she graciously agreed to talk with me. I wanted to understand her process of healing, whether and how her feelings changed over time. She was honest and open about her experiences.

When she first got home from Kansas, Carly was very selective with whom she shared her experience and only talked to close friends and family. She felt a lot of shame about her decision to end the pregnancy and was worried that she would be judged, which would have been too difficult to bear in her initially fragile state.

Over time, Carly has come to feel comfortable with her decision. She now recognizes that although it was a difficult one to make, under the circumstances and with the information she had, it was the right one. Though she once wondered whether she was a terrible person, she now feels at peace. She fully accepts herself and her decision.

With the passage of time, "it's not nearly as present . . . I go weeks without thinking about it, depending on the time of year." For years she and her husband had a ritual on December 27, the day Eli's heart stopped. But recently, there have been a few December twenty-sevenths where nothing has been said or acknowledged.

Despite my gentle suggestion to defer pregnancy to allow time for healing, Carly and her husband decided to get pregnant again right away. Her thoughts were: "If I wait too long, I'm worried that I'll be too afraid to try again. Let's keep moving and deal with the rest later." She was pregnant with her daughter within four months.

She relied on her knowledge as a genetic counselor to reassure herself during the pregnancy that all would be well. "I was dead set on being hopeful." Despite these positive thoughts, there were still fears. She says that when she gave birth, "It was almost like I couldn't believe we would have a live baby. My only (prior) experience of having a baby was one that was dead."

Carly now has four living children, and while she and her husband have come to terms with their decision, they are now facing the question of what to tell their growing children. Their children know that their parents lost their firstborn, but, for now, Carly and her husband have chosen not to share the circumstances. Instead, they focus on the loss and their sadness surrounding it, feelings that ebb and flow but have softened with the passage of time.

Carly has a special box containing Eli's things, including a blanket and a medallion, that she has stashed away in a closet. She told me she hasn't opened the box in a while. It's still too painful for her. Hearing that, I was reminded of what she said at the beginning of our conversation, that it was a difficult decision, but it was the right one.

And, if I live another eighteen years after this week's patients go home, I hope they, too, can tell me that for them, it may have been a difficult decision, but it was the right one.

PART TWO

CHAPTER 13

Fetal Indications

Women and families are intellectually, emotionally,
spiritually, and ethically competent to struggle with
complex health issues, including abortion, and come
to decisions that are appropriate for themselves.

—GEORGE R. TILLER, MD

Over the years, I cared for many patients in the third trimester. I saw people of every race, religion, and age and from all economic and educational backgrounds. My experiences taught me that behind every person is a story and that every story is unique. My patients' stories helped me to understand what led them to have an abortion. They also helped me to answer many questions that those not involved in abortion care often ask. Even some of those who support abortion rights are challenged by the notion of third-trimester abortions. Isn't some fixed gestational limit necessary at some point? Isn't adoption a viable alternative, especially in the third trimester? And, by far, the most common question is, why did she wait so long?

I am always glad to answer these questions, to explain the all-too-real circumstances of people's lives that do not fit into circumscribed gestational limits and preconceived notions. There are always answers.

Let's start with the simple question: "Why did she wait so long?" An implicit assumption underlying this question is that women have consciously decided to wait, to delay having an abortion until the third trimester when they could have easily made that decision earlier. It assumes an almost idealized scenario: A woman finds out she is pregnant at six weeks. She knows right away that she needs and wants an abortion and knows of an abortion clinic in her neighborhood. She has financial resources to pay for an abortion, or, if she has limited financial resources, she lives in a state that accepts Medicaid for abortion care. She can take time off work and arrange affordable childcare during the procedure. Her partner is supportive. She can have either a five-minute in-clinic procedure or an at-home medication abortion. However, instead of following through on this plan, she decides to wait another twenty-two weeks just so she can have a third-trimester abortion. In all my years of practice, I never met this woman, for either maternal or fetal indications.

Although many can understand those who seek an abortion for a severe fetal anomaly, especially a lethal anomaly, they still wonder why the patient didn't seek an abortion earlier in the pregnancy. What about all the early testing that is offered to patients, including blood tests and, often, multiple ultrasounds?

These questions presuppose access to quality healthcare and early prenatal care—not an assumption one can make in the United States where, despite the greatly expanded access provided by the Affordable Care Act (ACA), healthcare is still not universal.[1] Currently more than twenty-seven million people in the US do not have any health insurance, and 43 percent of adults aged nineteen to sixty-four are underinsured.[2] Given the haphazard care that many uninsured and underinsured people receive, one can understand a delay in care, a subsequent delay in the diagnosis of an anomaly, and a delay in the ability to access an abortion.

The second crucial consideration is the nature of the anomaly itself, which is not always clear cut. Some are lethal, incompatible with life, although the moment of death is uncertain. Death can occur in the womb, at birth, a few days later, or perhaps even a little longer afterward. The impossibility of knowing with any certainty is distressing for many patients and is a factor they consider when deciding whether to end the pregnancy. Other anomalies are nonlethal but may result in a level of disability that parents feel is overwhelming and unbearable. After consulting with experts, doing their own research, and talking to others, they may conclude that their child would not have an adequate quality of life, even under the best possible scenario. Or they may not have the physical, emotional, and financial capabilities to parent this child. These are some of the most difficult decisions imaginable, and they need to be understood through the eyes of the parents who face them and not through legislators or judges.

Louise's story provides insight into the challenges of how and when someone decides to end a pregnancy with a lethal anomaly. It exposes the difficulty of accessing care in a country that does not provide universal health insurance, and it illustrates the impact of abortion stigma precluding necessary, timely care.

LOUISE

Louise, a thirty-year-old Black woman from Texas, was excited to finally meet her midwife for her first prenatal appointment. She had been waiting for this appointment for months, ever since she found out that she was six weeks pregnant after missing a period. She wanted to access prenatal care right away, as she had with her first two children, but this time was different because she did not have health insurance. During her previous pregnancies, she had a full-time job with good health benefits. However, since the birth of her second child, she had left her job to stay home to care for the two young children, both under five years old. Her husband, Aaron, the family breadwinner, had gotten a new job recently and they were both waiting for his health insurance, which would cover the whole family, to kick in.

Everything had gone perfectly with her last two pregnancies and births. There was no reason to suspect that anything would be different this time. But something, Louise wasn't sure what, didn't feel quite right. She was twenty-three weeks pregnant when she finally met her midwife, who would attend her birth at a local hospital. At this initial visit, her midwife reviewed her medical and surgical history. Louise had hypertension, high blood pressure, which had developed after her last birth, but it was well controlled with the medication she was diligently taking. They talked about how hypertension put Louise at higher risk for preeclampsia, a disease of pregnancy that can lead to seizures, major organ damage, and death and that is seen at much higher rates in Black women. The midwife felt that, given her higher risk, Louise would benefit from transferring her care to an obstetrician. But first, she ordered some routine blood tests and an ultrasound.

Aaron was disappointed that he couldn't take time off from work for this first visit, but he was determined to be with Louise during the ultrasound. The ultrasound department was backlogged, and the soonest she could be seen was two weeks later. That seemed okay to Louise, especially since she was scheduled to meet the obstetrician one week after the ultrasound appointment.

Aaron took off work, and they arranged with Louise's mother to watch the children. They checked into their hospital's ultrasound department and were called into the darkened exam room by the ultrasound technician. While Aaron sat in a chair beside her, Louise lay flat on an exam table as the tech squeezed cold gel onto her belly, placed the ultrasound probe, and began the scan. At first, the tech was chatty, but then she became silent as she continued scanning. "Is anything wrong?" asked Aaron. Rather than answer the question, she responded, "I'm going to step out for a moment and call in the doctor," and quickly left the room.

Clearly, something *was* wrong, and Louise and Aaron waited with dread for the doctor to come in. A perky-looking doctor, whom they later described to me as looking like she wasn't more than twelve years old, walked in and, with the briefest of introductions, started intently scanning. Finally, she stopped, turned the lights on, had Louise sit up, and said, "I'm sorry to tell you that your baby has anencephaly, a lethal anomaly. I suggest you schedule an appointment with your healthcare provider as soon as possible to discuss this further." Then she left the room. At that very moment, Louise realized they were not going to have a baby.

Louise and Aaron were astounded. What was happening? How did a regular ultrasound appointment turn into a nightmare? What was anencephaly, and what did it mean that it was a lethal anomaly? Louise wondered whether she had done anything or thought anything to cause this, but how could that be? She didn't smoke or drink, and she started taking prenatal vitamins as soon as she realized she was pregnant, many weeks before her first prenatal appointment. Her other two children were the picture of health. How could this one not be healthy?

They were both in shock. Aaron stopped driving several times on the way home so they could cry and then compose themselves. Their most immediate concern was what they were going to tell Louise's mother when they got home. What were they going to tell the kids, who were young and barely grasped the concept that they were going to have a sibling? And *then* what were they going to do?

They decided to say nothing for the time being until they had more information. They went home and pasted on forced smiles. Louise's mother knew her well enough to sense something was amiss but knew better than to start interrogating her daughter.

After she left, Aaron and Louise started scouring the internet to learn as much as they could before their appointment with the obstetrician. They found out that anencephaly is a type of neural tube defect (NTD). Neural tube defects are the second most common congenital anomaly after heart defects but are the most common that I encountered in my practice, occurring in one in three thousand live births. When the neural tube, the structure that goes on to form the brain and spinal cord, doesn't close normally, an opening is left in the tube. The type of anomaly and subsequent disability mainly depends on the location as well as the size of the defect. As with Mary and Christopher's baby, who also had a neural tube defect, the tube didn't close properly. But in Louise and Aaron's case, the defect was in a different place.

If the defect is located high in the neural tube, the cranial portion, where the embryonic brain is forming, it can result in anencephaly. In that situation, part of the skull that normally protects brain tissue does not develop, and the brain is exposed to amniotic fluid, the bag of water that surrounds the pregnancy. The exposure of the unprotected brain to amniotic fluid leads to degeneration and destruction of brain tissue. Anencephaly is incompatible with life.

Anencephaly is incompatible with life. This is the sentence that Louise kept reading over and over again. She also found out that anencephaly is an anomaly that could have been diagnosed by ultrasound in the first trimester, but she was unable to access care earlier while waiting for her insurance to kick in, and she was now in the third trimester.

Even before the consultation with the obstetrician, Louise realized that her options were extremely limited. She could either continue the pregnancy to term, give birth, and she and Aaron could be with their baby as the baby died, or she could end the pregnancy now. If she continued the pregnancy, perinatal hospice might be a possibility if her local hospital provided it. Perinatal hospice is offered to patients whose babies have lethal anomalies, including anencephaly. This option involves the patient continuing the pregnancy to term, giving birth, and the hospital offering only comfort care to the baby until it dies.

When perinatal hospice is available, it can be a good option for some parents. However, going through childbirth is much riskier for a pregnant woman than abortion. The last time the mortality rate for abortion was calculated was from 2013–2019. (It is calculated over a seven- year period because the rate is so low.) That rate was 0.43 per 100,000.[3] In the same year, 2019, the overall maternal mortality rate for women giving birth was 20.1 per 100,000, and it was strikingly higher for Black women, at 44.0 per 100,000.[4]

The higher risk of mortality and the higher risk of preeclampsia for Black women are differences that are not due to imagined race-based genetic variations but *are* indicative of the grave impact of systemic racism on Black women's health. Clearly for Louise, continuing the pregnancy would put her life at greater risk than ending it. And although Louise recognized the significant risk to her health were she to continue the pregnancy, this wasn't her main concern. When Louise explained to me why she rejected hospice and decided to end the pregnancy, the safety of abortion compared to childbirth wasn't paramount. Her concern for her physical safety paled in comparison to more painful emotional issues—a shared characteristic among the women I saw in similar situations. For those whose babies will die at or shortly after birth, the idea of holding their child as it dies is excruciating. As Louise later explained her decision to me, "I didn't want him to open his eyes and then watch him die." And when perinatal hospice is not an option, parents worry that, as sometimes does happen, decisions will be taken away from them and their baby will be subjected to multiple painful interventions before their ultimate, untimely death.

The day before their obstetrician's appointment, Louise and Aaron talked to their families. By then they had decided to pursue an abortion and were unsure how the conversations would go, especially with Louise's mother, who was a churchgoing, God-fearing Christian. But to their surprise, her mother, who had her suspicions since they returned from the ultrasound, embraced Louise and extended her wholehearted support. Both sets of family offered to help in any way possible.

Given that positive response, they expected to receive a similar kind of support for their decision from the obstetrician. They anticipated that he would quickly make arrangements for Louise to have an abortion at the local hospital. In fact, although the doctor appeared sympathetic, he did not agree with that plan. Despite numerous restrictions on abortion care in Texas at the time, including gestational limits, there *was* an exception for severe fetal abnormalities, and anencephaly certainly fell into that category. However, there wasn't a single doctor in his practice who would perform abortions, either on what they considered to be moral grounds or for fear of community censure. Louise and Aaron would have to look elsewhere for care. When they asked the doctor where they could go, he mumbled something about New Mexico, wished them luck, and left the room.

Louise and Aaron were astounded. How could this be? How was it that neither their doctor nor others in the practice would care for them? Why did they have to leave their state to get care? It felt sneaky and illicit. They were attempting to obtain medical care for a legal procedure that would preserve Louise's health and end a doomed pregnancy. Why did they feel like criminals?

Once again, they went back to the internet to pursue the clue about New Mexico the doctor had shared with them. They googled "third-trimester abortions, New Mexico" and found Southwestern Women's Options in Albuquerque. They learned that in addition to the cost of the abortion, they would need to make arrangements to be there for a multiday procedure.

Ironically, and in another awful twist of fate, Louise, who had waited many weeks for insurance to kick in before starting prenatal care, now found out that her insurance would not cover abortion care. However, insurance *would* cover the costs if she assumed the increased risks to her health by continuing the pregnancy, gave birth at term in a hospital, and waited for her baby's inevitable death.

Our clinic's phone counselor, Sue, could sense Louise's worry and anxiety rising when she started to talk about logistics and costs, and she did her best to allay them. Sue told her about abortion funds that would help with the fee and, since they were planning to drive, funds that could provide money for gas. Once they were in Albuquerque, the New Mexico Religious Coalition for Reproductive Choice (NMRCRC)[5] would put them up in a hotel and provide them with food.

It was now Thursday. Sue told Louise that as long as all the arrangements were made, she could be seen the following week, starting on Tuesday morning at 7:00 a.m.

Louise and Aaron spent the next few days putting everything in place. Both sets of parents were going to share childcare. Aaron had to ask for time off work for a family emergency. Sue helped them contact the available abortion funds and offered them a no-interest loan from the clinic. They scrounged together the balance.

Monday arrived, and they started the long drive to Albuquerque. In the past, they had enjoyed long car rides. This one felt like one long nightmare. They were sad and angry, and angry and sad. They felt so alone, as if it was just the two of them against the whole world. It was during the trip to the clinic that Louise felt the spirit of the baby leaving. His heart wouldn't stop beating until the next day when the abortion process began, but by the time they reached the city limits, she felt as if his soul was gone.

Their time in Albuquerque was a blur. The abortion was the smoothest part of their ordeal. By Friday, they were back on the road, looking forward to giving and receiving many hugs from their children. They went home saddened yet satisfied that they had made the right decision.

Louise was stymied by her initial lack of health insurance, but even those patients lucky enough to have good insurance coverage and good prenatal care can find themselves seeking an abortion in the third trimester. The realities of prenatal testing and women's lives are complicated. We do not live in a world where there is universal early testing that picks up *all* abnormalities with 100 percent accuracy. In that fantasy world, women would also be given, and have access to, all options, including abortion. Instead, we live in a world where early testing does not and cannot detect all abnormalities, and legal abortion is either unavailable or threatened even at the earliest gestations.

Before Covid and the diminishing trust in science among significant swaths of the country, people believed in tests, yet even the most accurate tests are never 100 percent accurate 100 percent of the time. Tests can be wrong, and tests can get lost or misread. The inaccuracy of tests, or the human error involved in administering testing and interpreting test results, can be understandable, although the consequences are grave for the patient.

One patient I cared for knew she was a carrier for a disease that could cause severe intellectual disability in males. Before learning about this mutation, she had a healthy daughter, but she didn't want to take a chance with her second child. She had in vitro fertilization (IVF) with preimplantation genetic testing that would be able to determine the baby's sex, in addition to screening for genetic abnormalities. She was told that they had implanted a female. She had an ultrasound in the second trimester that noted a male; however, she was not informed of this until the third trimester. The ultrasound report said, "Patient thinks it's a girl." When she was finally told, she had further testing that revealed that a male with the full mutation had been implanted.

The stories patients told me, individually and in the fetal-indication group, about their experiences leading them to have an abortion in the third trimester rather than earlier in pregnancy often came out in bits and pieces. They were still in a state of shock, forced to come to terms with the unexpected and forced to make difficult decisions. Often, these decisions were made over time, bit by bit, as information shifted and changed. The story of Erika and her husband, Garin, a couple I met who had a third-trimester abortion at another clinic, illustrates this reality. They described to me the step-by-step incremental process that led Erika to have an abortion at thirty-one weeks.[6]

ERIKA

In the first trimester, Erika was referred by her ob-gyn to a maternal-fetal medicine (MFM) specialist for chorionic villus sampling, testing of early placental tissue for chromosome abnormalities. Having recently experienced a miscarriage, Erika was relieved that the results were normal. When she was fifteen weeks pregnant, only days after getting this good news, her ob-gyn called with bad news. One of her blood test results was markedly abnormal, a result that is almost always associated with poor pregnancy outcomes. She referred Erika right away back to the MFM specialist for further testing and evaluation.

Erika and Garin met with him the very next day. The doctor agreed that the abnormal test was concerning, but he was not as concerned as their ob-gyn. In his vast experience, he had seen miraculous outcomes. All they needed to do was to return every two weeks for an ultrasound. There was no need to panic.

They left the office feeling comforted by the doctor's reassurance. If they just did what they were told, it would be okay. If complications came up, they would deal with them. They would keep pushing forward. It all seemed, if not great, at least manageable. And thus began the roller coaster of emotions that so many of my patients described, as they alternated between hope and despair.

Every two weeks they took the trip to the doctor's office for another scan, and at every scan, something new was noted. First, one foot seemed abnormal, then both. Then it was determined that they both were clubfeet. Then the hands were clenched. Then the baby barely moved. The baby was growing, but not normally. There was a little too much fluid around the baby. It seemed scary, but they kept going with the reassurance and hope that the doctor offered. Finally, at thirty weeks, the ultrasound showed a dramatic increase in fluid and a dramatic decrease in the baby's growth. This baby would not survive. There was no longer a manageable, correctible, best-case scenario. Dejectedly, the MFM, who had appeared to Garin to be completely invested in their hope, referred them out of state for an abortion. It was now over four months since the original markedly abnormal test result, and they had passed the gestational limit for abortion in their state. It had taken that long to come to a definitive diagnosis, time that did not take into consideration the politics of abortion care.

In contrast to a step-by-step gradual recognition of anomalies that parents and providers have been aware of all along, some abnormalities are only diagnosed late in the pregnancy. Skeletal dysplasia (dwarfism) is an example of this, with some types being lethal. And some conditions can occur late, for example, a brain hemorrhage—bleeding in the brain that causes a fetal stroke. This condition is often lethal, but when not, it often results in severe intellectual and physical disability. There are also conditions that can worsen with time, transforming a mild anomaly into a severe one, changing a seemingly manageable situation into an unmanageable one. Hydrocephalous (excess fluid in the brain) is the most common example. And not uncommonly, diagnosing one anomaly leads to further testing that reveals more and more severe anomalies.

More nefarious is the provider who is anti-abortion and withholds information about all options when revealing the diagnosis, no matter how serious. One woman found out that her baby had a lethal type of dwarfism when, at thirty weeks gestation, she went for a nonmedical keepsake ultrasound. Although these ultrasounds are nondiagnostic and touted purely as mementos, the ultrasound technician noted and notified the woman of an increased amount of amniotic fluid. Armed with this information, she pressured her doctor for another ultrasound, this time at a medical facility, which showed a huge discrepancy between the size of the limbs and the size of the head, diagnostic of dwarfism. The doctor worked at a Catholic hospital that didn't offer abortion as an option. She told the patient: "Having a special needs child happens. I have a five-year-old with autism." And that was the end of the discussion. This doctor could not or would not move beyond her own personal experience and values to offer appropriate information and options to her patient whose baby had a lethal anomaly.

I listened to patients angrily tell me they were convinced their doctors intentionally delayed telling them about abnormal test results until the gestational limit for abortion in their state had passed. Patients also told me how betrayed they felt when their long-term doctors threatened to stop caring for them if they sought an abortion. Patients who were not well supported by their doctors during a time of crisis were particularly angry. They were angry and upset that their baby was sick and that they were not getting the medical care and guidance they needed from their own healthcare provider. Instead, they were left to search on the internet for a clinic that could care for them.

In rare contrast, I once cared for a patient who spoke about her referring doctor in glowing terms and who felt well cared for by her. The beauty of this was that the patient had *no* idea that her doctor was anti-abortion. I learned this only after the patient's care was completed and I made a routine follow-up call to her doctor. The doctor was happy to hear that all went well. She let me know, though, that while she did not personally believe in abortion, she always supported her patients' decisions. After I hung up the phone, I wondered, "Why can't more doctors be like her?"

Of course, delayed care following a diagnosis is not always the result of an anti-abortion doctor withholding information or guidance. Sometimes patients are left to find a clinic on their own due to providers' lack of knowledge about abortion options later in pregnancy or their incorrect assumptions about their patients. The provider may assume that a particular woman is not interested and, in fact, might be insulted if abortion is raised as an option. What if the woman is an evangelical Christian? What if she wears a burka or hijab? What if she is deeply conservative and anti-abortion? Doctors and genetic counselors who offer options following a diagnosis of a fetal anomaly may hesitate to talk about abortion with these women. And yet, I have cared for them.

Sometimes it takes time to make or confirm a diagnosis. It takes time to get more information, and it takes time to come to a decision. Often, when a fetal anomaly is diagnosed, the pregnancy is highly desired, and the fact that there is an unexpected problem is devastating. Commonly, when faced with a fetal anomaly, patients will seek a second and maybe even a third opinion. More testing will be done. As time passes, the gestational limit in their state may pass, as happened to Erika and many other patients I saw. The disjuncture between wanting to get as much information as possible, taking time to deliberate about the possible consequences of continuing the pregnancy, and the increasingly narrow gestational limits or outright bans in many states leads to a harrowing situation for many patients. An already difficult decision becomes even more so due to political realities.

COMING TO A DECISION

Whether a pregnancy is viable—as defined by the mother—is the issue for every abortion. Fetal-indication patients view viability in both the short and long term, depending on their circumstances. For patients like Louise and Erika, who learn that their unborn child cannot survive outside the womb, there is no long term. Their choice is between a safer abortion procedure and a more dangerous, and often more emotionally challenging, birth.

However, for those with a severe nonlethal anomaly, the factors to consider rapidly expand. There are immediate as well as longer-term considerations that lead to a decision as to whether a pregnancy is viable or nonviable. For many fetal-indication patients I cared for, the prospect of their child facing prolonged hospitalizations, multiple surgeries, intensive or lifelong care, and the uncertainty of the child's quality of life is intolerable. But this doesn't make the decision to pursue an abortion any easier. Among fetal-indication patients, the most difficult and painful decisions are often abortions for nonlethal anomalies.

Whether a fetus appears healthy or whether it has been diagnosed with a lethal or nonlethal anomaly does not factor into my decision to care for a woman seeking an abortion. What is important to me is to know that the woman has considered what is best for her, the child she is carrying, and her existing family. *Her* life and *her* life experiences, not any theoretical outcomes, shape her decision, and this is true for both fetal- and maternal-indication patients.

During my many years as an abortion provider, I learned that every woman who comes to me for an abortion has considered many factors relating to her, her unborn child, and her family before coming to her decision. Both fetal- and maternal-indication patients ask the same questions: Given the reality of my life, would I be able to care for this child? What would the quality of my child's life be once born? How would having this child impact my life, and how would having this child impact my other children's lives?

I learned that the decision to end a pregnancy for a fetal-indication patient is only partly about what she has learned about her baby's anomaly through testing and consultations. If not for the anomaly, most of these patients would not seek an abortion. However, the anomaly, in combination with a multitude of other factors, determines whether it is viable for her to continue this pregnancy.

I trust my patients' wisdom to determine what is best for them and their families, and I support their decisions. Just as I do not believe in a hierarchy of desperate circumstances when it comes to granting or not granting exceptions to abortion bans and restrictions, I do not believe in a hierarchy of severity of fetal anomalies to determine whether a patient deserves an abortion for fetal indications.

Every patient comes to a decision based on their life experiences. This decision is highly subjective by definition. For that reason, it should not be regulated, nor should it be judged. Three patients who exemplified the significance of life experiences in their decision-making were Dolores, Nancy, and Susan. And while Susan's case may initially invite puzzlement, as it did for me, further examination leads to understanding and compassion.

DOLORES

Dolores, a Latina in her thirties, had previously given birth to a baby with hydrocephalous that was diagnosed only after her birth. That baby died before her third birthday, after prolonged hospitalizations and multiple surgeries. One year after her child's death, Dolores was ready to have another child. She was delighted that she got pregnant so quickly. Because of her previous circumstance, she was being followed closely by an MFM specialist. Sadly, mild hydrocephalous was diagnosed at twenty weeks. She was advised to have follow-up ultrasounds to see whether the hydrocephalous would remain stable or would progress. If it continued to be mild, she would continue the pregnancy. But unfortunately, at twenty-six weeks, an ultrasound showed that it had increased significantly. It was no longer mild; it was now severe. Dolores did not want this child to undergo what her last child went through. She had a visceral understanding of the reality of treatment and care and decided to end this pregnancy.

NANCY

Nancy, a white woman in her early forties, came to see me after her baby was diagnosed with Angelman syndrome, a genetic condition causing severe intellectual disability. She already had a ten-year-old with the same disability. Taking care of him was more than a full-time role, and she had quit her paying job to take that on. Her marriage had not survived the stress. Despite marriage counseling, she and her husband divorced when her child was two years old. Her social world had narrowed down to herself and her child. Despite all the challenges in her life, when she found herself pregnant, she considered continuing the pregnancy. However, genetic testing revealed that this child would have the same disability. How could she care for two severely disabled children? She was doing the best she could under very trying circumstances and realized that she could not do more. After waiting for testing results and after much deliberation, she decided to end this pregnancy, despite now being in the third trimester. Had she not already had the experience of raising a disabled child on her own, and if she had the support of universal healthcare, childcare, and a supportive community, she may have made a different decision.

SUSAN

Susan, a white woman in her twenties, came to see me after an ultrasound revealed that her baby had a large cleft lip and palate.

Looking more closely at Susan, I could see the hint of a scar above her upper lip, signs of a surgical repair. As it turned out, Susan had been born with a cleft lip and palate, as had her father. At first I was perplexed. The defect had been successfully repaired. Why would she want to end this pregnancy because her baby had this same defect?

Susan explained that she had struggled throughout a childhood of multiple hospitalizations and over thirty surgeries to fix her cleft palate. Not only was the physical recovery arduous and painful, but Susan was also socially ostracized. She often had to miss school, and when she was there, classmates bullied her because of the way she looked. She felt that she had missed out on her childhood. By the time she reached adulthood, the surgeries were behind her. The physical scars had healed beautifully; yet despite years of therapy, the emotional ones lived on. She was adamant that what she had gone through was the kind of deep suffering she didn't want her child to inherit.

Susan was the only patient I encountered who had the same anomaly as her baby. She had a firsthand knowledge of her child's future, or at least what she thought it might be, that was based on her own experience. Perhaps most parents who learned while pregnant that their child had this diagnosis would have made a different decision, and perhaps, if Susan's baby had a different anomaly from hers, she, too, would have come to a different decision. But Susan's decision stemmed from her lived experience and not from anyone else's.

After spending time with Susan, I could care for her without judgement because I understood that, as with all my fetal- and maternal-indication patients, she deeply wanted to spare her child what she believed would be a life of pain and suffering. My decision to proceed with her abortion was based on her conclusion that this pregnancy was nonviable.

I am not an advocate of abortions for disabilities. Instead, I care for each person who comes to me who has made the careful decision to end a pregnancy after she has weighed all the factors that go into *her* decision. My job is not to judge. My job is to provide a safe abortion in a safe environment.

I understand the legitimate concerns of some disability rights advocates who maintain that abortions for fetal indications signal a disregard for the lives of those with disabilities. The history of forced sterilization of people with disabilities in the United States highlights this disregard.[7] But I also see how these concerns have been weaponized by the anti-abortion movement in a continuous effort to restrict or ban abortion care. Since 2010, a number of states have introduced and passed what have been called "reason-based abortion bans," bans on abortions for reasons of race, sex, and disability.[8] Eight states have enacted "disability-selective bans," which typically ban abortions for trisomy 21 (Down syndrome), though not for a myriad of other syndromes and anomalies that can occur.

Most nonlethal anomalies and syndromes, including Down syndrome, result in variable levels of disabilities that cannot be predicted through prenatal testing. However, in my experience, parents are acutely aware of this fact and weigh all the factors that allow them to make the best decision for the child, themselves, and their families. Some are willing to accept any possible outcome, hope for the best, and continue the pregnancy, while others do not want to rely on best-case scenarios and decide to end the pregnancy based on the information they have obtained. (This presupposes the ability to access an abortion, an increasingly tenuous assumption in many states.)

I respect all of these possible decisions, while proponents of these bans do not. Although these bans are purportedly enacted for the protection of children with disabilities, it is notable that these bans are not accompanied by legislation that provides funding for services and assistance to children and adults with disabilities. To me, it is clear that, as with any abortion restriction that claims to value life, these bans value the life of the disabled fetus and not the life of the disabled person once born.

Supporters of disability-selective bans support the trope that parents who end a pregnancy for fetal indications are seeking the "perfect" baby, unable to cope with life's imperfections. However, in all my years of practice, I never met a patient who expressed those beliefs. On the contrary, I have cared for patients who were prepared to care for a baby with a severe anomaly but reconsidered only after further testing revealed additional abnormalities. What motivated them was not the quest for the "perfect" baby, but rather a tenacious desire to spare their child a lifetime, however short, of suffering.

When another of my patients, Desiree, an Asian American, learned that her baby had a large meningomyelocele, a neural tube defect similar to that of Mary's baby, she was undaunted. Her baby would be at high risk to never be able to walk nor have bladder or bowel control. Nevertheless, she was planning to continue the pregnancy and told me that "I would carry her on my back if I had to." But then, unrelated to this defect, further testing revealed a massive bleed in the baby's brain, a fetal stroke. In addition to her physical disability, Desiree's baby would have minimal to no cognitive function. At that point, she concluded that "I want what's best for my baby" and decided to proceed with an abortion. She named her child Journey, honoring the journey the two of them had been through. She was a devout Christian, and she absolutely knew that God was right beside her, guiding her and supporting her. Her faith in God led her to tell me before she travelled home, "I hope that God continues to help you to do the work that you do."

Both disabled and able-bodied people have abortions. Like able-bodied people, people with disabilities come to a decision to end the pregnancy after considering the many factors affecting their lives, including access to healthcare. And, as with the able-bodied, they currently face restrictions and bans that limit access, requiring out-of-state travel. Travel may be onerous for people with mobility issues or those requiring time-sensitive treatments, making an abortion all but impossible to access.[9]

The particular challenges that people with disabilities face highlight the importance of supporting all decisions surrounding pregnancy. No one, disabled or able-bodied, should be denied an abortion because of lack of access. And no one, disabled or able-bodied, should be denied the opportunity to continue their pregnancy. Either decision requires a respect for bodily autonomy and a government committed to providing adequate resources for all.

The foremost lesson I learned in my career is this: Patients come to a decision based on the reality of their lives, not an idealized version of their lives. What guided me in my work as an abortion provider was a deep, and ever deepening, appreciation and respect for patients' abilities to decide what is right for them and their families.

CHAPTER 14

Maternal Indications

I am having this procedure because my husband was
tragically killed before I knew I was pregnant. I was
suddenly thrust into being a single mother to our two
other children and I couldn't do it alone. I do not
regret this. I already have the two best parts of him.

—ANONYMOUS PATIENT

Tonya was a thirteen-year-old Black girl from Chicago, with small
features and a big belly. She sat facing me on the clinic couch in
the private waiting room, huddled beside her much larger mother,
Tamara, who enveloped her like a mother bird with her chick.
Before meeting Tonya, I read what she told the phone counselor
before coming to the clinic. What stuck in my mind was this:
"What fears me the most is that I'm young and I still need my
mom and I don't know how to be a mom."

Between the two of them, I heard the story of the events that
had brought them in. Tamara was a single parent who had given
birth to Tonya when she was sixteen years old. She was determined
to give Tonya a better life than hers, and she set about making it
happen. Tamara worked two jobs, slept little, and trusted that
Tonya would manage on her own after school until Tamara came
home for a few hours of rest before going to her next job.

Gradually, however, Tamara noticed that Tonya's behavior was
changing. She had been loud, rambunctious, and energetic. Now,
increasingly, Tonya was quiet, withdrawn, and lethargic. She had
once answered questions eagerly, at length, in full paragraphs.

Now, she responded in monosyllables. At first, Tamara attributed these changes to normal teenage development. Then she noticed that Tonya, who had always loved to dress up, was wearing baggy clothes. This was all so mysterious. Tonya still hadn't had a period. Could she be pregnant?

Under intense questioning, Tonya admitted that rather than coming home straight from school, she had been "hanging out" for months with a seventeen-year-old boy from the neighborhood. Or at least that's what he told Tonya, and in her thirteen-year-old naivete, that's what she believed. But when Tonya said his name, her mother knew him to be a forty-one-year-old man who preyed on girls in the neighborhood.

Tamara took two actions. Despite having little faith that anything would come of it, she reported him to the police, who picked him up and charged him with statutory rape. More pressing for the immediate future, she went out and bought a pregnancy test. It was positive.

Tamara asked Tonya what she wanted to do. There were three options, as far as she could see: Tonya could have the baby, and the two of them could care for the child together. She could have the baby and relinquish it for adoption. Or she could have an abortion. Tonya said that she wanted an abortion. She was sure about that.

Later, when I spoke to Tonya privately to ensure that she was seeking an abortion without coercion and to see whether there was anything else she wanted to tell me without her mother present, I asked her to say more about how she was doing and about her decision. These last months had been so confusing, she said. Her body kept changing, and she didn't understand why. What was the fluttering she was feeling in her belly? Why was it so hard to keep up with all the other girls at basketball practice? Her best friend said that kids at school were talking about her and were spreading rumors that she was pregnant. That was just not possible. But when she looked at the pregnancy test with her mother, she finally knew the truth. And she also knew that she could not stay pregnant for one more day.

Seeing how hard her mother worked to pay the rent every month and put food on the table, it was clear to Tonya how difficult it would be to be a single parent. And she had dreams. First, she wanted to finish high school. She proudly told me that she was an honors student and a point guard on her middle school basketball team. Eventually, she wanted to be either a pediatrician or a forensic investigator. (I kept hearing from teenagers that this was their career aspiration; it was the era of *CSI* and *NCIS*.)

And what about adoption? "If I gave it up for adoption, I will be wondering if it's being treated well, is its parent taking care of it, is it being fed?" she told me.

Tamara called the one abortion clinic in their area and made an appointment for the following week. After an ultrasound to see how far along Tonya was, the tech spoke to Tonya and Tamara. Staring coldly at Tonya, she said, "We can't help you. You're too far along. Have a good time shopping for baby clothes." At that point, Tonya started sobbing.

Thanks to the internet, Tamara found a clinic that could care for her thirteen-year-old daughter—our clinic in Albuquerque. Thanks to abortion funds and practical support provided by reproductive justice organizations, the cost of the abortion was covered. Tamara and Tonya were assisted with transportation to and from the clinic and with housing during their time away from home. And thanks to Tamara's fierce love for Tonya, she got the support she needed to have a safe abortion.

At her checkout exam, Tonya wore a bright smile to match her bright, tight clothes. She felt confident that she had made the right decision. Over a year later, I got a card from Tamara. She wrote that Tonya had started therapy as soon as they got home to process all that she had been through. She was thriving, studying hard, and once again keeping up with the other girls at basketball practice. She thanked all of us at the clinic for saving her daughter's life.

In contrast to the patients who seek abortions for fetal indications in the third trimester because their baby is unhealthy, Tonya's baby was presumably healthy. Her reasons for seeking an abortion were for maternal indications, which cover a wide range of situations. Maternal-indication patients may be young like Tonya and may not be ready on any level to have a baby or parent a child. They may be victims of rape, domestic abuse, or both. They may have serious medical conditions and have been advised that childbirth could be life threatening. They may be addicted to drugs or alcohol. They may live in poverty and cannot afford to raise a child. They may have educational and career aspirations that would be impeded by trying to raise a child before they are ready. A number of these factors may be true for any of them.

These are many of the same reasons that patients would seek an abortion in the first or second trimester; however, my third-trimester patients have faced additional difficulties, internal and external barriers that prevented them from accessing care earlier in pregnancy. Those circumstances may be hard for others to understand. While many people feel compassion for fetal-indication patients who discover that their baby has a life-threatening anomaly in the third trimester, many have negative judgements about maternal-indication patients who come for care late in pregnancy. These are the patients for whom the question—*why did she wait so long?*—often arrives with judgment or exasperation.

However, as I worked with these patients and heard their stories, I came to understand some of the complexities of these patients' lives and to admire how they navigated difficult situations to make the best decisions they could for themselves and their families. Like fetal-indication patients, maternal-indication patients have looked at many factors and circumstances in their lives and wrestled with the question of whether it is viable to continue their pregnancies. As with fetal-indication patients, there are many reasons why maternal-indication patients may seek an abortion, and many reasons why they may not seek or be able to access abortion care until the third trimester. It is usually a confluence of factors, with reasons encompassing all the complexities of women and their families' lives and situations, including poverty, domestic violence, rape, drug and alcohol addiction, and youth. Teenagers face distinct challenges and obstacles to accessing care, including parental consent laws. Additionally, there have been multiple restrictions and bans on abortion enacted throughout the United States, which have the effect of delaying or preventing women of all ages from accessing care.

There are better questions to ask instead of *why did she wait so long?* And the answers to these questions should inspire compassion rather than judgment. What were the barriers to abortion care the patient faced when confronting an unwanted pregnancy? What were the life circumstances that compelled her to seek an abortion in the third trimester? In this chapter, I'll share stories that answer these questions.

NORMA

Norma, a Black woman from Louisiana, was in her mid-thirties. She was a single parent of a twelve- and a fourteen-year-old and had her hands full. She worked long hours for low pay as a nursing assistant at a long-term care facility. She also helped her mother, who lived a few houses down the block, care for her husband, Norma's father, who suffered from advanced dementia. Norma was managing, but it was a struggle every month to pay the rent and feed her kids. She couldn't rely on her children's father, who was in prison on drug charges, to pay child support.

Norma had a long-term, long-distance relationship with a trucker who she saw when he was in town. She was taking birth control pills and used them reliably until the month she ran out and couldn't afford to buy a new pack. That was the month that her boyfriend unexpectedly came home. Norma realized she was pregnant almost the minute that she conceived. She wasn't overjoyed when the pregnancy test confirmed her suspicions, but she also wasn't distraught. She talked with her mother and boyfriend and reviewed the likely impact of another child on her life and family.

For Norma, there were several issues to consider. One of the biggest issues was financial. How could she afford to care for another child while barely managing to care for the two she already had? She also wondered what it would be like to start all over with a newborn. Her children were finally becoming independent, and she had been looking forward to having a little time to pursue a better-paying job.

Furthermore, the fear of pregnancy and childbirth loomed. Twelve years prior, when she last gave birth, she had hemorrhaged badly and required multiple blood transfusions. It was a scary experience, and she felt that it contributed to the postpartum depression she experienced afterward. Her doctor told Norma that she was at risk for another hemorrhage in a future delivery. What he didn't say was that Louisiana has one of the highest maternal mortality rates in the country, with Black women in the state having a four times higher risk of a maternal death than white women.[1]

Norma's mother promised to help with the baby, and her boyfriend encouraged her to continue the pregnancy. As much as he liked her two kids, he was excited by the prospect of having his own child and pledged to support her. With a small degree of apprehension and a large amount of hope, Norma decided to continue the pregnancy and have another child.

The early months of the pregnancy were hard. Norma suffered from severe nausea and vomiting. She quickly used up her limited sick leave and had to miss days of work without pay. Thankfully, her symptoms abated as she headed into the second trimester. She was just starting to feel well when her mother had a stroke. It was relatively mild, but unless she improved dramatically, it seemed unlikely that Norma would get much help from her mother with the baby. On the contrary, if she continued the pregnancy, she would have to take care of the baby, her two kids, her mother, *and* her father with dementia. How could she handle all of this? It seemed overwhelming.

Without telling her mother or boyfriend, Norma made an appointment for an abortion. This was pre-*Dobbs* decision, and abortion was legal at the time in Louisiana, although with many restrictions. One of the restrictions was a twenty-four-hour waiting period, meaning she would have to make two visits to the clinic, the first for counseling and an ultrasound, the second for the procedure.[2] She would have to dip into her meager savings to pay for the abortion, as Louisiana Medicaid does not cover abortion. And once again, she would have to take time off work without pay. The first visit was uneventful. On the way to her second visit, her car broke down along the way. Norma took this as a sign that she wasn't supposed to have an abortion, and after calling a close, trustworthy friend to pick her up, she went back home, determined to make the best of things. And she did, running ragged for months on very little sleep, working extra hours to make up for the days she had missed and would miss after the birth, taking care of her kids and her ailing parents, still hoping that with her boyfriend's support, everything would work out. For a while, it did—and then it didn't.

Her boyfriend, by now her only dependable source of support, was killed in a trucking accident. Norma was devastated and grieved his loss deeply. She had tried to make the pregnancy work, but given the circumstances of her life, the pregnancy now had ceased to be viable.

Norma thought long and hard about her options. She realized that a broken car on the way to an abortion clinic was not a sign that she wasn't meant to have an abortion. It was only a sign that she was too poor to buy a reliable car. She called the clinic again but learned that she was too late to have an abortion in Louisiana. Thankfully, that clinic referred her to Southwestern Women's Options in New Mexico. She spoke with the very kind counselor, Sue, over the phone, and together, they worked out all the financial and logistical arrangements so she could be seen.

Perhaps her decision would have been different and having another child would have been a viable option if she had lived in Norway, a country in which parents are entitled to generous paid leave.[3] But she lived in Louisiana, the third-poorest state in the country, with the fourth-highest rate of maternal mortality. It was a dangerous state to birth a child in, and if she continued the pregnancy, there would be minimal support for her, the baby, or her two other children.

Similar to the situation of some fetal-indication patients, the circumstances of maternal-indication patients may change over time. Erika and Garin, fetal-indication patients who we met in the last chapter, learned early in pregnancy that their baby had an anomaly, but they were hopeful until the news progressively worsened. Similarly, maternal-indication patients may also decide to end their pregnancies only after a series of events that transform a viable, or somewhat viable, pregnancy into a nonviable one, as was the case with Norma. Yet the exigencies of time often do not align with restrictive abortion laws.

EVA

Many maternal-indication patients I saw faced severe challenges in their lives that made it impossible for them to access care earlier in the pregnancy. Some were trapped in situations of abuse. Some were locked in a state of post-traumatic stress after a sexual assault. Others were not able to think beyond the demands of their addiction to drugs or alcohol. Poverty also contributes to the difficulty of accessing care in a timely manner.

Reflecting the national statistics of abortion patients in *all* trimesters, the majority of patients I cared for were living in poverty.[4] Some were unhoused, often couch surfing or living in shelters or on the streets. Those who were housed were often living precariously, barely eking by. The disaster of an unwanted pregnancy under difficult social circumstances was exacerbated by their financial instability, and being able to get to a clinic and pay for an abortion was extremely problematic. This was the case for Eva, whose housing was precarious and tied to an abusive partner.

Eva was a twenty-three-year-old white woman from a small town in Texas. She had three children ranging in age from two to seven and was married to her high school boyfriend, Bo. When she first found herself pregnant at sixteen, she dropped out of high school and moved into Bo's tiny apartment. Bo started physically abusing her at the end of that pregnancy, and despite his claims that each episode was the last, the abuse never stopped. Every time Eva made plans to leave, she got pregnant and had another child. At first, she hid the abuse from her family, but eventually, she confided in her parents, who believed and supported her and urged her to leave. But it was hard. She was immobilized by fear of the unknown. How could she manage with her children? Where would they live? Nevertheless, by the time she got pregnant for a fourth time, she knew that to save her and her children's lives she had to end this pregnancy and make plans to leave. But she didn't know how. As much as she tried to hide the pregnancy from him, Bo figured out that she was pregnant and the abuse intensified. Eva felt desperate and trapped. Suicide briefly crossed her mind, but she didn't want to leave her kids without their mother.

Her salvation finally came when Bo was picked up by the police for a parole violation and put in jail. As soon as that happened, her parents swooped in and took her and her children into their home. The next day, her parents drove her to the closest abortion clinic, the Boyds' clinic in Dallas, but by then, she was in the third trimester, which was too late to be cared for in Texas. The Dallas clinic referred her to Southwestern Women's Options in New Mexico. While her parents took care of the children, she made the trip to Albuquerque by herself, the first time she had been alone in years.

The violence Eva experienced was common among the patients I cared for. One week, all of the patients in the maternal-indication group, all teenagers, had been raped. Several shared stories of having no memory of the assault and of the confusion of trying to understand their bodily changes over the months. Because of the trauma of their assaults, they had suppressed the memories of the incidents and had become completely disconnected from their bodies.

The patients I cared for who were addicted to drugs or alcohol also frequently experienced this disconnection with their bodies. Their struggles to cope with their addiction took precedence over all other concerns. Nonetheless, I was always impressed that they were eventually able to see through the fog of addiction, realize that they could not care for a child, and decide that abortion was the best option for them. I heard more than once that they did not want their child to suffer because of their addiction, and if they were considering adoption, they were concerned about prospective parents who would have to care for a drug- or alcohol-exposed child. Frequently, they were considering entering a rehab program but were refused entry while pregnant. For these patients, ending the pregnancy gave them an opportunity to go to rehab and potentially change their lives for the better.

DIANE

Many of the maternal-indication patients I saw experienced the powerful strength of the coping mechanism of denial. When my wife, Julie, was trying to get pregnant, we were exquisitely attuned to all the minute bodily changes that were possible with a pregnancy. When she successfully became pregnant, we noticed the profound changes that pregnancy brought day by day, month by month. However, Julie *wanted* to be pregnant, and she embraced these changes.

This was far different from my patients. I heard countless women lament later, "How could I have been so stupid?" They might have noticed their belly growing, but they thought it was because they stopped working out and were eating more junk food. They might have missed one or a few periods but told themselves they often had irregular periods. They might have been using birth control or have been told they were unlikely to get pregnant, which led them to ignore or find other reasons to explain away all the signs of pregnancy.

In contrast to this conscious denial, I often saw an unconscious manifestation of denial as the woman's body adapted to an unwanted and hidden pregnancy. On the day of the patient's arrival at the clinic, she presented to us as she presented herself to the world. She did not look very pregnant, if at all. By the second day, once the abortion was in process, she looked completely different. Her belly was protruding, and, finally, she allowed herself to look pregnant because she knew that soon she would not be. I began to understand this phenomenon when I saw a maternal-indication patient walk into a room filled with other maternal-indication patients on day two, look around, and say, "Well girls, doesn't it feel good to breathe again and to stop sucking in your stomach all the time?" They all laughed nervously, perhaps finally able to acknowledge what they had been unconsciously doing for so many months.

I also vividly recognized denial when I met Diane, a young Asian American woman. She came to the clinic accompanied by her boyfriend, Andy. Both were seniors at a large university in Texas and had been dating since they met at a fraternity party their freshman year. Diane had a history of an irregular cycle and was used to missing periods. She didn't think that she could be pregnant even when she started missing more periods than usual. She didn't look pregnant, and she didn't feel pregnant. One day, Melanie, her best friend, confided to Diane that she felt pregnant but was too scared to check. To lower Melanie's anxiety, Diane suggested that they both take a pregnancy test together. To their surprise, Melanie's test was negative, but Diane's was positive.

Andy and Diane agreed that this was not a good time to have a child. They were both students, focused on their studies and financially dependent on their parents. Diane was taking a rigorous course of study, about to get her degree and apply to graduate school. If she continued the pregnancy, their families would pressure them to keep the child. Diane would have to drop out, derailing all her plans. They decided an abortion was the best decision for them. But an ultrasound showed that Diane was too far along in her pregnancy to be cared for in Texas, and she was referred to New Mexico.

When I met Diane, she told me that she and Andy were still perplexed that she was pregnant, and even more so that she was in the third trimester. Yes, she had the "flu" several months ago and threw up for days, but that went away. Her clothes still fit. Everything felt the same to both of them.

In the middle of the night on the first day of treatment, after the medication had been administered to the fetus to stop its heartbeat and after the laminaria were placed, Andy, in a panic, called the clinic from the hotel where they were staying. He said that Diane was "all swollen." He and Diane were convinced that something wasn't right. Despite the late hour, I asked them to come see me at the clinic for an exam. Everything checked out normal. What was swollen was Diane's uterus, which was just the right size for her gestational age. Now that the abortion process was underway, she and Andy could finally both acknowledge and recognize the profound bodily changes that had been occurring all along.

Diane and Andy perhaps exhibited an extreme example of denial, but it was common for a patient to tell me that she couldn't be pregnant because she didn't look pregnant. Upon examining her, however, I encountered a clearly pregnant belly that wouldn't require an ob-gyn to diagnose.

It is not the case that these patients were any less knowledgeable or sensitive than others. Rather, for these women, coping with an unintended, unwanted pregnancy was so frightening and inconceivable that the only response was an unconscious one, to retreat to a bearable state by not acknowledging the pregnancy. This was the case for Diane.

ELLIE

Symptoms of denial are especially common in teens and preteens, who comprised a significant number of the third-trimester maternal-indication patients that I cared for. I had an affinity for these young women, whose situations were unusually difficult and who, by virtue of their age, faced additional barriers to accessing care, sometimes leading to third-trimester abortions. Some, like Tonya at the opening of this chapter, were naïve and were mystified and perplexed by their bodily changes. Others like Noor were stymied by the abortion restrictions that all patients face, overlaid by the restriction of parental consent laws.

Parental consent laws were among the first restrictions to be placed on abortion following the 1992 *Planned Parenthood of Southeastern Pennsylvania v. Casey* decision, which also allowed mandatory informed consents and mandatory waiting periods from the time of signing a consent to the abortion. Thirty-six states require parental involvement in a minor's decision to have an abortion, either through consent or notification.[5] These restrictions are moot in the states that have banned abortion since June 2022 when *Roe* was overturned but were in full force when I was in practice.

New Mexico did not have parental consent laws, but Texas, the largest neighboring state, did, and I cared for many teens who crossed the border for an abortion. Although all states with this restriction offered an opportunity to circumvent it through court approval, known as a judicial bypass, over time, the process for approval became more onerous. In Texas, by 2005, parents were not only required to be notified, they also were required to give consent, and in 2006, the consent had to be notarized. Then, in 2016, the judicial bypass system in Texas grew even more restrictive, becoming practically nonexistent. Judges now had to be from the county where the patient lived if its population was greater than ten thousand. Escaping to the anonymity of a big city to go in front of a judge was no longer an option. Additionally, the number of judicial bypasses a judge issued now became public record. Given that judges are elected officials, the chilling effect was clear. The tighter the restrictions in Texas, the more teenagers I cared for in New Mexico.

Ellie, a Texan, was a seventeen-year-old Latina who came from a religious family. Her mother had told her that she would not speak to her if she came home pregnant. Given that admonition, telling her parents was not an option when she found herself pregnant. She sought a judicial bypass. She was denied and was told it was because she hadn't considered adoption. She told the judge that she had done a lot of reading, had considered adoption, and had rejected it. Nevertheless, he told her that she wasn't mature enough to have an abortion, and her application was denied. She logically asked him, "How can you say I'm not mature enough to have an abortion and yet be mature enough to carry a pregnancy to term and care for a child?" The judge stared at her and didn't respond. She contacted Jane's Due Process, a group that helps Texas teenagers access the judicial bypass system and arrange care outside the state if it is denied.[6] They helped her make the arrangements to come to New Mexico for care, the only neighboring state that does not have parental consent laws. But because of the delays in setting up the judicial process and making arrangements to leave town without arousing her parents' suspicions, Ellie was early in the third trimester by the time I saw her.

Ellie was bright, had a lot of initiative, and managed to leave the state to get an abortion when her judicial bypass was denied in Texas. I always wondered and worried about the girls left behind. What would happen to them? Would *they* be able to go to college and become pediatricians as Ellie dreamed of? Would *they* be able to care for themselves and the children they already had? Or would they be stuck in what Dr. Tiller called "the dungeon of mandatory motherhood"?

Invariably, whatever their background, the teens I have cared for were often very high achieving girls. Often, they were straight-A students, excellent athletes, involved in an untold number of extracurricular activities. They had high expectations for themselves, as did their parents. They were often close to their parents, more so to their mothers. Nonetheless, over and over again, girls told me that they hid the pregnancy because they were afraid of their parents' imagined reactions of disappointment, anger, sadness, or all three. They wore baggy clothes and carried on with their lives as if nothing was wrong. I can't imagine how difficult this time of knowing and holding this growing secret must have been. If asked whether they could be pregnant, they said no.

This was a source of bewilderment and confusion for their mothers. "She tells me everything. We have a good relationship. Why couldn't she talk to me about this? I always told her to let me know if she needed birth control." When parents brought this up in the group for support people in Kansas, Reverend Gardner, who led the group, responded, "You weren't with her when she got pregnant, were you?" His point was that even in the closest families, some things are private.

Even in states that do not have mandatory parental consent or notification laws, delays in seeking an abortion because of the teenager's denial, fear, lack of information, and lack of resources means that the pregnancy advances and parental help is invariably needed. Eventually, reality breaks through, either because the mother forces the issue or the girl finally speaks up. One nineteen-year-old told me she was afraid to tell her mother until one day her mother asked her, "Are you pregnant? I had a dream last night about a fish, and it was a really big fish."

Teens often lamented to me, "I can't even take care of myself. How can I take care of a baby?" Others told me of their and their family's dreams and aspirations for them—of a better life, of education, of a career. A twelve-year-old from a small town in Mississippi told me that she had known many pregnant girls and girls with babies. She could see how hard it was for them. I asked her what her dreams were. She said, "My grandmother [who she adored] told her friend that she dreams that I'll finish high school."

I wanted this girl to fulfill her grandmother's dreams and begin to develop her own. I believed in her and her ability to forge her own path, unencumbered by a pregnancy that was not viable for her. I felt honored that I could help her on her journey.

What was remarkable about the maternal-indication patients I cared for was their ability to overcome all the obstacles put in front of them to access an abortion. Some were legislative barriers like gestational age limits and parental consent laws. Some were societal barriers like poverty and domestic abuse. And some were internal, like denial. By the time patients came to the clinic, they had pushed through these barriers. They knew that abortion was the best decision for them and their families.

CHAPTER 15

Adoption and Safe Haven Laws

I don't think that I would get over it,
putting it up for adoption.

—ÁNONYMOUS PATIENT

If the most common question I'm asked about third-trimester patients is, *Why did she wait so long,* then the second most common
is this: *Why doesn't she just give the baby up for adoption?*

This question is usually asked regarding maternal-indication
patients, especially teens who, as far as is known, are carrying a
healthy baby. Many people think that if a woman is already in the
third trimester, it would be little trouble to give birth and relinquish
the baby. Indeed, the further along the pregnancy, the more often
adoption is raised as *the* solution to unwanted pregnancies.

However, in many cases, this is a simplistic view of a complex
situation. Although adoption is an option for some, it is not for
others. When faced with an unwanted pregnancy, there are only
three options to consider:

1. Continue the pregnancy, give birth, and raise the child.
2. Continue the pregnancy, give birth, and relinquish the
   child for adoption.
3. End the pregnancy.

Options one and two incur the risks of childbirth. Although
the risks of childbirth as compared to abortion are not the most

important reasons that my patients gave for not wanting to continue their pregnancies, it must be acknowledged how much riskier childbirth is than abortion, especially for Black women, as Louise's story illustrated.[1]

The patients I cared for were an admittedly self-selecting group who were able to access an abortion. From reviewing the phone intakes and talking to patients, I could see that they had very carefully considered adoption and ruled it out as an option for themselves. Overwhelmingly, by the time they came to the clinic, if they couldn't have an abortion, they would continue the pregnancy and parent the child.

My anecdotal findings are corroborated by *The Turnaway Study* led by Diana Greene Foster. The landmark study compared the outcomes of women who had abortions and those who were turned away because they had passed the clinic's gestational limit. Foster was intrigued by the low rate of adoption among those turned away. One week after being turned away, only 14 percent of women were considering adoption, and, ultimately, only 9 percent followed through. In other words, 91 percent of women who were unable to obtain an abortion decided to continue the pregnancy and parent their child.[2] And what did that mean for their and their children's lives? *The Turnaway Study* found that, compared to women who were able to access an abortion, women who were forced to give birth and chose to raise the child had higher rates of poverty and an inability to meet basic needs, including food and housing. They were more likely to be unemployed. They were more likely to stay with their abusive partner. The children they already had were more likely to live below the poverty line and less likely to achieve developmental milestones compared to the existing children of women who had abortions.

At the end of the week, after seeing the relieved face of a patient at her checkout exam, I often wondered what might have happened to her if she *hadn't* been able to access an abortion. Would she have been in the majority, continued the pregnancy, parented the child, and faced the possible consequences of *The Turnaway Study*'s findings? Would she have been among the fewer than 10 percent who would have relinquished the child for adoption? Or would she have taken more desperate measures?

Dr. Tiller described the impact of relinquishing a child as "cutting off an arm and being able to function afterwards but always being aware that your arm is missing and wondering what happened to it." Over time, through talking to patients and reading, I have come to understand and appreciate that perspective, as do my patients.[3]

TARA

Tara was a twenty-four-year-old white woman. She was working at Walmart, earning minimum wage but hoping to study to become a nurse.

When she was fifteen years old, she became pregnant. After she told her parents, they said her that she was too young to be a parent and that they were neither financially nor emotionally equipped to care for a baby at this stage of their lives. They decided that the best thing for her was to relinquish the child for adoption. Her parents also decided that, in order to avoid the inevitable judgment she would face in school and in her town, they would send her away until after the birth.

Tara dropped out of high school and went to live with her aunt. Although close to her aunt, she remembers feeling extremely lonely, isolated, and bored during that time. She was away from her friends, her parents, and her town. She felt like a reject and an outcast. Meanwhile, her parents made the adoption arrangements, and she signed the required papers.

Tara described the birth and the immediate postpartum period as a distressing and horrifying experience. She felt that no one paid any attention to *her* needs. Worried that she would feel attachment to the baby, she told the labor and delivery nurse attending her that she did not want to see the baby after the birth. Rather than listening to Tara, the baby was kept in a bassinet in the room with her for hours. She felt trapped in the room, with no escape. As her daughter started crying, Tara felt compelled to pick her up to comfort her. This was exactly what she had wanted to avoid because, as she held her baby, she experienced deep feelings of connection. By the time her daughter was taken away, Tara was distraught.

Since that time, Tara has had occasional contact with her biological daughter, mainly through photos. She feels a great sense of loss, and, in retrospect, regrets the adoption. Although she recognizes that she was too young to be a parent, she feels that she was coerced. She wishes she had been given two different options: parenting or abortion.

Ever since that birth, Tara's life has been off-kilter. She never went back to high school, although she eventually earned a GED. When she turned eighteen, she got pregnant again, this time from a short-lived relationship. Although life was hard, she was determined to parent the child, another daughter.

By the time I saw her, she was pregnant for the third time. Initially, she considered continuing the pregnancy and parenting the child. When she told the man involved, who was unemployed and addicted to methamphetamines, that she was pregnant, his response was "Do what you need to do." She realized he could not be relied upon for any kind of support. Once again, she would have to parent on her own. She also didn't think she could rely on her parents. She imagined they would judge her as irresponsible for getting pregnant when she couldn't care for another child.

Tara was deeply attached to the daughter she was already parenting. All of her focus was on caring for her and providing for her as best she could on her minimum wage job. She was trying to save money to take prerequisite classes for nursing school so that the two of them could have a better life. Eventually, when her life was more secure and she had more support, she would consider parenting another child. But right now, caring for another child as a single parent would be a financial disaster. What kind of life would she be able to provide for her children? Yet because of her personal experience with adoption, she believed that relinquishing another child would be a worse solution.

Contemplating adoption brought up all her past traumas—of being sent away when she was pregnant, of the hours after birth with her crying baby, of her lack of agency every step of the way, and, most importantly, of her deep sense of loss. She could not tolerate that kind of loss ever again.

In this pregnancy, her decision was between parenting and abortion. Tara carefully and deliberately weighed her options and decided it would be best for her to proceed with an abortion. Financial and logistical challenges slowed her down, and she was too far along to receive care at a clinic close to home. Like so many others, she was referred to Albuquerque. This presented new challenges. How could she take off time from work and still pay the rent? Who would take care of her daughter when she had to leave town for a week? She reluctantly turned to her parents for assistance and was surprised that they supported her decision and offered to care for her daughter while she was away.

Tara had a traumatic history with adoption. But not everyone who rejects adoption has had a personal experience. Every person who comes to see me has their own story and their own decision-making process. For some, the circumstances of *this* particular pregnancy are the determining factors.

DEXTER

Dexter, a white trans man, was twenty-eight years old. Since breaking up with his girlfriend over a year ago, he had been celibate and rarely socialized. His work friends decided it was time for him to start going out again and one Friday insisted that he go with them to an after-work party at a coworker's home. After much cajoling, he agreed.

The party was loud and raucous, filled with many people Dexter didn't know. Generally a teetotaler, he had one drink. He remembered that at some point he lost track of his friends and started to look for them. The next thing he remembered was being in a bedroom, feeling disheveled, pulling his pants up, and tucking his shirt back into his pants. He felt disoriented and confused.

Since starting testosterone hormone therapy several years prior, Dexter had rarely had periods. One day, he felt fluttering in his belly. The sensation felt unusual but not worrisome. He told a girlfriend, who encouraged him to take a pregnancy test. Dexter thought that was ridiculous. He couldn't be pregnant. He was a man! Still, he agreed to check with a test and was shocked to see that it was positive. He was confused and immediately scheduled an ultrasound at the local Planned Parenthood. There he learned that he was pregnant in the third trimester.

When Dexter did the math, he realized he had gotten pregnant at the party. Someone must have slipped a drug into his drink and raped him.

As soon as Dexter put the pieces together, his relationship to his body, which had previously been one of pride, shifted dramatically. He felt intense disgust. It felt like there was an evil monster, an alien, inside him who had invaded his body. He felt he had to get it out as soon as possible.

In a recovery room notebook, he wrote: "My body will not tolerate the presence of a child—something in my mind won't allow it. It's like a body snatcher." This idea—that his body was possessed of an evil being, a parasite—isn't a unique one. I have spoken to many women with undesired pregnancies who feel the same way. The idea of continuing the pregnancy for even one more minute is intolerable to them. Dexter, like other survivors of rape, wondered how anything good could come out of such a heinous act. There was no question in his mind that he needed to end this pregnancy, and much to his relief, he did. For Dexter, ending the pregnancy and ridding his body of what he saw as the evil within was essential for his emotional survival. Continuing the pregnancy, giving birth, and relinquishing the baby for adoption was in no way a viable option.

MONIQUE

For Monique, a Black college student, abortion was the only option because pregnancy was simply not; it would have derailed everything. Monique was a college basketball star on an athletic scholarship. She was the first person in her family to go to college, and she was determined to succeed. Despite the demands of the sport, she was maintaining an A average. Following graduation, her dream was to play basketball professionally. And after that? Perhaps sports medicine. Every game in which she excelled and was noticed by WNBA scouts was bringing her closer to her dreams.

All of that changed when she realized she was pregnant. The mere spotting, the missed periods? Monique attributed those signs of pregnancy to the stress of competing on such a high level and the constant travel to games. She explained her weight gain as being due to a poor diet, eating too much junk food when the team was on the road. When she started to get out of breath running down the court, something that had never happened before, she finally decided to check a home pregnancy test.

Monique knew she had to have an abortion as soon as she saw the line on the pregnancy test. There was no doubt in her mind. To continue the pregnancy, to give birth even with plans to relinquish the baby for adoption, would end her life as she knew it and everything she had planned. Her athletic prowess had allowed her to go to college and would hopefully allow her to have a successful career. If she continued the pregnancy, she would not be able to play basketball. If she could not play, she would lose her athletic scholarship. She would not be able to finish college, and her hopes for a career in basketball and beyond would be destroyed.

Patients' decisions to have an abortion are often rooted in concerns for their own physical and emotional well-being and the impact of a child on their future. For others, although these concerns are present, what is foremost is their concern for their unborn child.

HEATHER

Heather was one of the first patients who showed me the deep concern my patients had for their unborn children and their fears about relinquishing them for adoption. She was a sweet, good-hearted, almost placid white sixteen-year-old from Alabama who was accompanied by her mother. As with Tonya and so many teenagers I cared for, she was a good student, intent on becoming a pediatrician. An introvert and an only child, she didn't socialize much. On weekends, she went to church with her parents and was involved in her church's youth group. There was a boy in the group she liked and they started hanging out together. She thought he was nice.

One Friday night, he invited her to go out to the movies. On the way home, they had sex in the back seat of his car. It was her first time. A few weeks later, when her period didn't come, she took a pregnancy test. She called the boy to let him know that her test was positive. He responded, "It's not mine," and hung up on her. He never spoke to her again.

It never occurred to Heather to tell her parents, and she didn't have the wherewithal to seek an abortion on her own. Her family was conservative and churchgoing. How could she ever admit to having sex before marriage, let alone to being pregnant? So in the typical fashion of teenage girls hiding their pregnancies from family and friends, she resorted to baggy sweatshirts and pants. Time went by. Her mother became suspicious and started asking Heather whether she could be pregnant. Heather denied and denied it, but she couldn't keep up the façade and eventually broke down and told her parents.

She was surprised by her parents' reaction, which was initially angry but then supportive of her desire to have an abortion. They knew of her strong desire to pursue her education and become a doctor, and they also knew she would be ostracized if she continued the pregnancy. They looked for a clinic nearby. So much time had passed that by the time she was seen, she had passed the Alabama gestational limit and was referred to our clinic.

I found Heather endearing. On the day she was to be induced she gave me a gift, a small ceramic angel. I put it in gurney, the room where patients labored, to watch over her and all the women that would follow her. I appreciated the angel, but the bigger gift was what she told me about her decision to have an abortion and not relinquish the baby for adoption. She said, "I don't want to do that because I've heard stories about women giving up their babies, and the children are mistreated. And I couldn't bear that. And, if I have an abortion—as cheesy as it sounds—it'll go to heaven."

Many patients after Heather expressed similar concerns, if not in quite the same language. They were worried about the life their child would lead if it was adopted, most commonly expressing worries that the child would feel abandoned, unwanted, or would be mistreated. One patient told me, "I don't feel that I can emotionally handle the pain of not knowing how safe it is, if it's in good hands with a different family or worrying or thinking about it for the rest of my life."

"The pain and the knowing that it's there and it's not there" was too much to bear for some. And many patients felt what this patient expressed: "You go through the whole process of carrying it and knowing it and you just give it away. Knowing it's still out there somehow and it doesn't know it was given away. That it was unwanted at the time, it was seen as a burden. I guess I don't think I'd be able to live with myself if I gave up a child. To think about me possibly living a good life while a child of mine is out there struggling."

A patient's partner, a Black man named Terence, described his concern for the kind of life his child would have if he and his partner relinquished it for adoption. As a Black boy in the United States, the child might well go through childhood without being adopted, with an uncertain future. As Terence told me bluntly, "We know this is a boy. What that would mean as an African American baby is that he would probably end up in foster care. It would be different if he were Asian American or Jewish. Then he would be adopted. And, yes, there are exceptions, but there's a good chance that he would end up in jail, on drugs. I work with high-risk youth. I know what his future would look like, and I wouldn't want that for him."

It is difficult to know what the life of the child relinquished for adoption would look like, and there are those who simply cannot go forward with the possibility that they are bringing a child into the world who might grow up unhappy, unwanted, lost.

CATALINA

Some parents choose abortion over adoption with the well-being of their unborn child in mind. Then there are those who worry about the impact adoption would have on the children they *already* have.

I hadn't thought of that until I met Catalina. She was a white woman in her early forties, a single mother of two children, ages eight and fourteen. She was managing but just barely. She could not afford to care for another child, yet she believed adoption was not a realistic option for her and her family. How could she explain to her kids that she wanted *them* and didn't want *this* one? How would it be possible for them to feel secure with her ever again? Would they worry that she might relinquish them as well? How could they not at least wonder?

Catalina was sure that, knowing about the adoption, one of her children would do everything possible to find their sibling and be part of its life. How would the adopted child feel? Would it grow up always wondering, "Why didn't you love me enough to keep me?" These questions plagued her and led her to decide to have an abortion.

SAFE HAVEN LAWS

A recent spin on the adoption alternative was presented during oral arguments at the Supreme Court during the *Dobbs* case that decided the fate of *Roe*. The newly appointed justice Amy Coney Barrett posited that the "burdens of parenting" could be obviated by safe haven laws, laws that were first enacted in Texas in 1999 after three cases of infanticide that year were highly publicized and sensationalized.[4] In the final decision overturning *Roe*, Justice Alito reiterated this sentiment in his majority opinion.

Abortion, Coney Barrett implied, is no longer necessary because women with an unwanted pregnancy can continue the pregnancy, give birth, then drop off the newborn baby at a designated location, often a fire station or a hospital, without threat of criminal prosecution for abandonment as long as the baby is healthy. From there, the baby will be placed in foster care, then put up for adoption as quickly as possible. Those who are not adopted will remain in foster care. Under these safe haven laws, when a birth mother drops off her child, she relinquishes all rights, unlike in a formal adoption process, where there may be a designated period in which she can change her mind. The adopted child will have no knowledge of its biological parents and no way to obtain what may be significant family medical history.

By now, all fifty states have adopted safe haven laws, albeit with different conditions. In eight states, babies can be relinquished up to seventy-two hours after birth; in nineteen, after thirty days; and in North Dakota, up to one year. Not all states guarantee anonymity, and some safe haven laws may clash with laws criminalizing concealment of a delivery.[5]

The problems with safe haven laws go beyond inconsistent state laws and regulations. These laws were a knee-jerk response to isolated cases of neonatal infanticide and did not actually address the common causes of infanticide, child abuse, and neglect. They were not enacted as an alternative to abortion, yet that is how they are now presented. In all my years of practice, when discussing options, not a single patient ever told me that if she was forced to continue the pregnancy she would drop the baby off at a safe haven location.

Now that there is less access to abortion after the overturning of *Roe* by the *Dobbs* decision, will there be more women who utilize safe haven laws? If the past is a predictor, most women who are denied abortions will go on to parent their children, doing the best they can, with minimal to no governmental support.

A few will take more desperate measures, like the cases of abandonment and infanticide that have occurred even in states with safe haven laws.[6] These tragic stories are the logical outgrowth of abortion stigma, fear, desperation, and a lack of options, including lack of access to birth control and abortion.[7]

For the women I cared for, it was clear that adoption was not the answer, but neither was parenting a child they could not care for. Abortion was the answer. Perhaps that is why, although I have wrestled with many questions in my work, the question of why she didn't just "give the baby up for adoption" was never one of them. I felt grateful that the patients I cared for were able to make the best decisions for themselves, for their particular lives, and in their particular circumstances.

CHAPTER 16

Endings

The cycle of life is a puzzling thing; birth, life, death. . . .
But, fate is fate. I look back on my choices and the path I
have made and think of the great distance I have travelled.
This step I will never forget. I tell myself, never forget.
Abortion isn't a crime. It's a choice all women have.

Rape victims as myself, homeless, jobless, and
widowed, we aren't evil, we aren't greedy. We are
fighting to survive . . . Last night I told myself the
stars shine for our lost ones, watching us.

Doing this makes you a strong individual,
not weak. It takes a lot of courage and faith
to follow through with this decision.

Be strong. Be free.

—ANONYMOUS PATIENT

By 2020 I had been traveling to Albuquerque every other week for
ten years. On Monday, I flew in. On Tuesday, I met frightened
and distraught patients and cared for them day and night for the
duration of the process. On Thursday and Friday, I said goodbye
to these now transformed individuals. And finally, on Saturday I
flew home to Oakland. I spent the week at home catching up on
sleep, on my life, and on my relationships with family and friends.
During the week of respite, it didn't take long for me to recover
from sleepless nights. By the following Monday I was ready to
start all over again. This schedule worked for me. Since beginning my employment with Dr. Tiller in Kansas in 2002, with a

few variations, it had been my life for almost twenty years, and I imagined it continuing in that same pattern for many more.

Then came the Covid-19 pandemic. I left Oakland for my week in Albuquerque on March 16, 2020, the week the governor of California issued the first stay-at-home order in the country to mitigate the spread of the virus. Residents could only leave their homes for essential tasks and were advised to keep six feet away from other people. All businesses considered nonessential were ordered to close, and their employees had to work from home. All nonessential gatherings of any size were prohibited, as well as nonessential travel. On my flight that day, the airplane was full, and no one was masked. It wouldn't be like that again for a long time.

To reduce the risk of exposure from being on an airplane, I stayed and worked in Albuquerque for four consecutive weeks. During that month, Albuquerque turned into an eerie and scary world. There were few cars and few people on the streets. Most stores were closed. And everything changed at the clinic. We were used to caring for anxious and frightened patients, but now all of the staff felt that way too as we waited for personal protective equipment to arrive. Early on we didn't yet know how the virus was transmitted, but clearly, the fear was airborne. A few staff members were so frightened that over the coming weeks, they took leave or quarantined and never returned.

We still had to care for patients, and we knew that because abortion is so time sensitive, patients would continue to come. We were committed to continuing to care for them as safely as possible, and the first week of the lockdown was especially busy.

The pandemic was yet another barrier that patients faced. Patients from Texas were particularly burdened by this. Following Texas governor Greg Abbott's edict that all medically unnecessary surgeries and procedures be postponed, the anti-abortion attorney general of Texas, Ken Paxton, mandated that abortion clinics close for a month, deeming abortion "not medically necessary." Meanwhile, liquor stores were allowed to stay open. Other states quickly followed suit and also closed their clinics. In a foreshadowing of the current situation, in which twenty-two states have either banned or restricted abortion care as of the time of this writing in August 2024, desperate out-of-state patients in all trimesters were forced to leave their states for an abortion. And this was in the midst of a pandemic in which the mandate was to avoid travel as much as possible.

The impact of Texas closing down all abortion services in the state was immediate. Even prior to the pandemic, we typically saw patients from Texas in all trimesters due to the state's numerous abortion care restrictions. The first- and second-trimester patients mostly came from Dallas and west of Dallas, an approximately nine-and-a-half-hour one-way drive. Pre-Covid, that seemed like a very long trip for an abortion. However, with the closure of all Texas clinics, we started seeing patients who had to drive all the way from Houston, a thirteen-hour one-way trip, or even further east.

Because they couldn't access care in Texas, some of these patients who were early in pregnancy needed to drive to New Mexico from Houston just to pick up pills for a medication abortion, the two-medication regimen that induces an abortion and is effective at least to eleven weeks. After their clinic visit, they immediately turned around and drove home. I marveled at patients' fortitude and determination while suppressing my rage. How was this cruel edict stopping the spread of Covid? Was it not the very definition of an undue burden to force women to travel such large distances in the midst of a pandemic? This temporary shutdown was the shape of things to come for Texas and, with the fall of *Roe*, the whole country.

Especially before the vaccine became available, the staff and I all worked in a state of semi-denial and fatalism. It was impossible to stay six feet away from a laboring patient. While I had my arms around a patient having a difficult time in labor who had thrown off her mask and was breathing deeply, I thought it would be miraculous if the staff and I didn't all get infected.

I kept working, but I was anxious. I wondered when I would be able to go home and what it would be like when I did. Once I made it home, how would I be able to turn around and return to work? What would happen if Julie and NoahLani got sick while I was in Albuquerque? What would happen if I got sick while I was in Albuquerque? What if I brought the virus home and infected my family?

The clinic I left four weeks into the pandemic was very different from the pre-Covid clinic. By then, all patients were wearing masks, mostly supplied by the clinic. Patients were encouraged to drive and not fly to Albuquerque. Those who flew were advised to stay quarantined, except to get to and from the clinic. They were discouraged from bringing any support people with them, and if someone did come with them, that person was to stay either in the hotel or wait in a car outside the clinic. Family members and support people could no longer sit in the waiting room. Seats were reserved for patients and were spaced six feet apart, as were the recovery room chairs.

At the end of those first four weeks, my flight home had only five passengers on it. Throughout the pandemic, I continued to fly back and forth between Oakland and Albuquerque. Before the vaccine and before anyone knew how the virus was transmitted, I stripped off my travel clothes and showered as soon as I came home, hoping to wash off Covid germs I might have picked up on the plane or in the airport. It was an ever-present risk that Julie and I were willing to take to allow me to care for patients. I felt scared and hopeless. Two months into the pandemic, I wrote in my journal: "Millions of people are out of work, people are starving, the death rate keeps climbing and there is NO end in sight."

Meanwhile, the political attacks on abortion were increasing. In September of 2021, SB 8, legislation called the "Heartbeat Bill," passed in Texas, banning abortions after the electrical impulses of the future fetal heart could be detected at approximately six weeks. It empowered citizens, rather than law enforcement, to sue providers or any person who helped a patient access an abortion in Texas after this limit. Just like during the temporary shutdown of abortion clinics at the onset of Covid, we began to see more and more patients from Texas after the passage of SB 8 and anticipated seeing more patients from Oklahoma and Arizona, as they, too, were poised to pass similar bans. The Supreme Court took up the *Dobbs* case, which would overturn the *Roe* decision, less than a year later.

I was exhausted. Though I had intended to work many more years, I began to contemplate retirement. I was worn down by Covid and all its attendant anxiety, the constant traveling, the cumulative fatigue, the difficulty of twenty-four-hour calls, and the constant political turmoil surrounding abortion. It was all adding up. It was time to stop and pass on my knowledge and experience.

When I first started providing third-trimester abortion care, there were only two providers of this care in the country, Dr. Tiller and Dr. Hern. Lee Carhart, Susan Robinson, and I were the second generation, and subsequently, over time, three more all-trimester clinics opened on the East Coast. Because of our collective determination to train new providers, there was a third generation. I realized it was time to stop practicing and let the next generation of third-trimester providers take over.[1]

By the time I retired, Carmen Landau, the first doctor Susan Robinson and I trained, had been working at the clinic for ten years. The plan was for her to take over as the clinic's medical director. Emily Cohen, the doctor Carmen and I subsequently trained, had joined the practice. Kalin Gregory-Davis, the licensed midwife who I met when she worked as a clinic counselor, had gone on to medical school and was planning to become an ob-gyn who would provide third-trimester abortions. She returned to the clinic for a rotation in reproductive healthcare that coincided with my last three months of work. Spending that final time at the clinic with Kalin felt like the circle had been closed.

I had sought out mentorship all along my path to becoming a provider of third-trimester abortion care. I was lucky to learn from the collective wisdom of Jim McMahon in Los Angeles, Kate Bowland in Santa Cruz, and finally George Tiller in Wichita. Each one of them taught me valuable lessons that served me well over the years. I never imagined that one day, I would be experienced and wise enough to play that role for others. Now, I was a mentor to Carmen, Emily, and Kalin. They were the new generation of third-trimester care providers. I could step away.

THE LAST ABORTION

It was December 10, 2021. I walked into the exam room to meet the patient, knowing she would be the last I would care for as an abortion provider. She was a delightful young woman in the first trimester who gave off the vibes of a California surfer girl, albeit in dry, landlocked New Mexico. In fact, she had grown up in a religious household but had left the fold.

The abortion was uncomplicated and went smoothly. I walked out of the room to check the pregnancy tissue in the lab to ensure that the abortion was complete. The staff, who were hiding in the lab, popped out and applauded me as I walked in. I returned to the patient, who had been warned by a staff member beforehand that she would hear clapping, and thanked her for allowing me to take care of her for my last abortion. She told me she felt honored.

I left the room, hunched over a table, and sobbed. These were tears of relief—relief that she had done well, that she could move on in her life, and so could I.

While I helped my patients transform their lives, they transformed my life as well. Years of spending time with patients taught me how to listen carefully and deeply. I learned that my patients were doing the best they could, often under very desperate conditions. They had concluded that, based on the circumstances of their lives, this particular pregnancy was nonviable, that it could not be sustained, that it needed to end. And I came to understand that this view of viability was deeply rooted in the reality of their lives, stripped of fantasy. I fully accepted that my job was not to judge. My job was to care for patients as fully as I could.

I continue to feel joy that, in my career, I was able to treat patients with—as my mentor Dr. George Tiller often said—kindness, courtesy, justice, love, and respect. I believe I made a difference in people's lives, that I helped my patients reach their full potential, that my work mattered.

With time, I came to realize that my commitment to this work is deeply rooted in my own experiences of the terror of an unwanted pregnancy. Of course, every situation is different, and my experience and motivations are different from anyone else's. From my personal feelings and experiences came political awareness. I believe that without bodily autonomy, women are extremely limited in what they can accomplish. Children deserve to come into a world where they are wanted, cherished, and can be cared for with adequate resources.

All that is true, yet at the core is my own experience of being a twelve-year-old girl who felt very alone, who needed compassionate care. This is what I hope I provided to the many patients I cared for. And this is why I became an abortion provider. Every day that I was at work confirmed to me the importance of providing safe and legal abortions. I cared for incredibly desperate women in very difficult circumstances. It never ceased to amaze and gratify me that abortion, a safe and relatively simple procedure, could give a woman back her life. Years ago, a patient said to me, "You know doc, you know how people say you're a baby killer? Well, you're a life saver. Now I can be a better mom to my son."

EPILOGUE

The *Dobbs* decision of June 2022, which overturned *Roe v. Wade*, dealt a profound blow to abortion care access in the United States. But it did not create the current patchwork of access. There already existed a multitude of laws and regulations in many states that severely limited care. *Dobbs* gave states that already restricted abortion, such as Texas, license and legal protection to further restrict or ban abortion. Other states, such as California, strengthened access to abortion in response to the decision.

The effect of the *Dobbs* decision and the climate surrounding abortion bans has been to extend the difficulties and challenges that so many of my third-trimester patients always faced to *all* women in states that now have free rein to limit or ban abortion. Some women with financial resources, or those able to tap into practical support organizations and abortion funds, will surmount the increasing number of barriers to accessing care.[1] But inevitably, there will be many who will fall through the cracks, and undoubtedly, those will be the most vulnerable and most marginalized, including Black and brown patients, people with low incomes, those living with disabilities, and teens.

The *Dobbs* decision ensures that women will die unnecessarily. Some will die in childbirth, and some will die after being denied emergency care for pregnancy complications.[2] Increasing numbers of women will be criminalized during pregnancy, and more families will barely scrape by without necessary resources.

What will the impact of forced childbirth be on those who can't access an abortion? We know they will face the markedly increased health risks of childbirth over abortion, and we can expect the maternal mortality rate, which is already obscenely high in the United States, to continue to increase.[3] We already know from *The Turnaway Study* that there will be negative long-term effects on their physical and emotional well-being, as well as on the well-being of their children.

The exclusive value placed on the unborn, but not on either the child once born or its parent(s), leads to laws that assign personhood to fetuses and embryos, the criminalization of pregnant women, and the denial of appropriate medical care for complicated pregnancies.

Most states that have banned abortions have exceptions for the life—but not the health—of the mother. But the exception is so vague that doctors and hospitals, afraid of prosecution, deny care to women in dangerous situations.

Recently, Kate Cox, a white woman, was denied an abortion in Texas despite a lethal fetal anomaly and advice from her doctors to end the pregnancy to preserve her health and fertility. She appealed her case to the Texas Supreme Court on the basis of medical exceptions, was denied, and was forced to leave the state to obtain care.[4]

Brittany Watts, a Black woman in Ohio, was arrested after miscarrying at home and being unable to dispose of the fetal body.[5] She was twenty-one weeks pregnant when her bag of water broke, too early for the fetus to survive. Instead of treating her appropriately by performing an abortion to end the pregnancy and prevent the possibility of infection, sepsis, and death, a hospital ethics committee denied her care and sent her home after eight hours of deliberation, where she then miscarried. After returning to the hospital because she was bleeding heavily, a nurse reported her to the police, who arrested her. A grand jury declined to indict her, but the harm to her was already done. Rather than being able to focus on grieving her loss, she was subjected to the trauma of arrest and possible prison time—all while her own health was at risk, yet ignored.

In response, twenty women in Texas who experienced situations similar to Kate's and Brittany's joined a lawsuit asking the state to clarify its laws on narrow medical exemptions and to put an end to the withholding of life-saving treatment. In May 2024, the Texas Supreme Court rejected their claims, stating that the medical exceptions in the law were broad enough and did not require further clarification.[6]

The Care Post-*Roe* study is currently documenting cases where the usual standard of care has been changed to adhere to laws that have much more to do with politics than with common sense and appropriate medical care. In the first six months of this still-ongoing study, researchers have documented fifty cases, many harrowing, where the change in standards led to delays in care and significantly worsened health outcomes.[7]

What these findings show is that Kate and Brittany are not alone. The situations they faced—complicated pregnancies—are not uncommon. Among lawmakers and many outside observers, there is a temptation to consider such women and their circumstances as rare exceptions. But I have learned in my career as an abortion provider, as an ob-gyn, and as a midwife that *every* pregnancy presents with its unique circumstances, some foreseeable and some not. Was it to be expected that after four rounds of IVF, Mary's baby would have a severe neural tube defect? That Irene's cancer would recur and mask the signs of pregnancy? That Norma's partner would be killed in a trucking accident? The challenge for providers when caring for patients when these situations arise is to treat patients competently and compassionately. It is not to deny or withhold care.

We live in a country that is punitive—one that is adept at criminalizing and incarcerating people while offering minimal to no support to those living with the consequences of these policies. An effect of legally assigning personhood to fetuses and embryos, which is a growing phenomenon, is that pregnant women are often treated with suspicion and are even criminalized. This was the case with Brittany. Across the country, and predominantly in five Southern states, pregnant women—overwhelmingly low income and disproportionally Black—have been jailed for suspected or actual drug use.[8] But rather than receive appropriate care, they are punished. This is a slippery and disturbing slope, as multiple activities—smoking, bungee jumping, skiing—could be seen as injurious to the fetus and deserving of prison.

The states that have banned or severely restricted abortion have not increased social services to support pregnant women and their families. Value is placed on the unborn, not on either the child once born or their parent. The result has been pregnant women facing prison time, the denial of appropriate medical care for complicated pregnancies, and the shrinkage of options for women and families.

The anti-abortion movement's drive to ban all abortion is unrelenting, and it is impossible to recount all the legislative measures to further restrict it, including penalizing out-of-state travel for an abortion under the guise of "trafficking" the fetus.[9] The laws that are being enacted now, as I write in the summer of 2024, will undoubtedly have changed by the time this book is published. Some will be dependent on the 2024 election results. Now that Donald Trump has been elected president, a fifteen-week federal ban on abortions will surely be considered, as well as a ban on mailing medication abortion pills, based on the 1873 Comstock Act that banned the mailing of "obscene materials."

Contraception is already under attack, and the Fifth Circuit Court of Appeals has upheld a Texas law requiring parental consent before teenagers can obtain contraception.[10] Parental consent laws were one of the first restrictions to be put in place on abortion care. If this ruling is a harbinger of things to come, then contraception for all who need it is at risk. Also at risk is IVF, as evidenced by the 2024 Alabama Supreme Court ruling that embryos created through IVF be considered "extrauterine children." The court ruled that Alabama's 1872 Wrongful Death of a Child Act be applied to frozen embryos.[11] While the Alabama legislature responded quickly by passing laws giving legal protection to IVF clinics, the court ruling demonstrates the logical consequence of assigning personhood to fetuses and embryos.

It is well known that banning abortions does not eliminate them. Desperate women will continue to do whatever they can to access an abortion, and current research bears that out. The Guttmacher Institute, the research organization that studies reproductive health, reports that despite bans in multiple states, the number of abortions in 2023 *increased* to their highest numbers since 2012.[12] While the number of abortions in restricted and banned states has plummeted, unrestricted states have noted huge increases in numbers. Banning or restricting abortions in certain states does not prevent them; women will travel to other states to obtain abortion services if they can't access them in their own state. They will take advantage of online resources to access medication abortion pills.[13] And if they cannot access a safe abortion through any of these resources, they will resort to dangerous methods to end their pregnancy, just as in the years before *Roe* when hospital wards were filled with women dying from unsafe abortions.

NEW PARADIGMS

Across the country, many voters have responded to the *Dobbs* decision by supporting the right to abortion. In August 2022, voters in Kentucky and in Kansas, Dr. Tiller's home state, rejected proposed state constitutional amendments that would have denied the right to an abortion in their states. During the midterm elections in November 2022, multiple races swung Democratic in response to *Roe's* overturning. California, Michigan, and Vermont passed ballot initiatives amending their states' constitutions to establish an explicit right to an abortion, while an anti-abortion bill was defeated in Montana. In the latest election cycle, in November 2023, voters in Ohio approved a constitutional amendment guaranteeing the right to abortion.

In these victories, I see the possibility of new paradigms after *Roe's* overturning. Some Democrats, including Joe Biden during his 2024 presidential campaign, speak of fighting to make *Roe* "the law of the land again."[14] But I do not believe that restoring *Roe*, with its multitudes of restrictions, is the answer to the current crisis in access to abortion care. *Roe* had many drawbacks, including the numerous limitations to care that were sanctioned over the years. Instead, the overturning of *Roe* creates an opportunity for an improved approach.

Abortion care should be recognized as a fundamental aspect of reproductive justice, a concept first introduced by Black feminists in 1994. Reproductive justice is defined as "the human right to maintain personal bodily autonomy, have children, not have children, and parent the children we have in safe and sustainable communities."[15] This framework places abortion care within the context of patients' lives and societal obligations.

In keeping with this vision, abortion care should be recognized as the essential healthcare that it is. Abortion is a medical procedure, and, like any other medical procedure, it should be available to those who need it. It should be regulated by experts in the medical field, not by the whims of politicians, legislatures, or judges. And such regulations should be enacted to maintain the safety of the procedure, not to create barriers to care. Such a shift recognizes that arbitrary gestational limits to determine viability are short-sighted and unreliable. It instead honors the wisdom of the pregnant woman to determine whether a pregnancy is either viable or nonviable. If there is one thing I have learned time and again throughout my practice, it is that each individual mother grasps—and grapples with—the viability of her pregnancy with far more knowledge, depth, and understanding than an outside policymaker can ever hope to.

For patients who *do* decide that their pregnancy is nonviable, they should have access to abortion care that addresses their physical, emotional, and spiritual needs, such as the care provided at Women's Health Care Services and Southwestern Women's Options. Furthermore, the care that physicians and clinics offer should encompass an understanding of each woman's individual situation as well as the societal pressures they face.

A model for this kind of care is exemplified by Valley Abortion Group in Albuquerque. It is a woman of color–led group of abortion doulas, counselors, and doctors that is committed to offering all-trimester abortion care within a structure that promotes economic, racial, disability, and gender justice, for both patients and staff. They anticipate opening this innovative clinic in the fall of 2024.

These new paradigms will allow us to move beyond *Dobbs*, beyond *Roe*, beyond limits—so that we can focus on the care itself and the people who need and deserve it.

ACKNOWLEDGMENTS

I recognize the sensitive nature of what I reveal about my personal story in this book and the impact it may have on others. It is not my intent to cause harm. However, it would be impossible for me to tell my story without shining a light on the kind of sexual assault that too often is shrouded in secrecy and shame.

It did not take a village to write this book; it took a megalopolis populated by professionals, colleagues, friends, and family, both past and present. There are many people to thank for their help and encouragement, and I hope to mention them all. This is very likely the only book I will ever write, so it's my one chance to thank everyone. If I've left anyone out, please forgive me. It's due to faulty memory rather than intent.

Without the support, love, encouragement, and editing skills of my wife, Julie Litwin, this book would never have moved beyond "the shitty first draft" that now sits on the upper left corner of my laptop. This is also true for our son, NoahLani Litwinsella, whose incisive comments always came at just the right time. My sister always stood by me, despite the challenges of this story.

My agent, Veronica Goldstein at United Talent Agency, has always been known to my friends as "Veronica, my agent, who I love." She provided encouragement and wise counsel even when this book was a mere idea. I am grateful for Dr. Willie Parker for making the initial introduction to Veronica. Many thanks to Haley Lynch, my editor at Beacon Press, for deciding that *Beyond Limits* was worthy of publication. Sofia Resnick helped with editing the proposal; Henry Ferris pointed me in the right direction; and Jon Cox did a tremendous job in helping to create the book's structure.

The rest of my acknowledgements will be, more or less, in chronological order. Larry Ceplair was the high school teacher who taught me how to think critically. He inspired me to attend the University of Wisconsin–Madison where I started my path toward providing abortion care and where I met my two closest friends, Fredda, my boss at the Madison Community Health Center, and Roni, who I met at the Main Course. At the time, we were effectively pluripotential stem cells. We've all grown and changed, and yet our bonds are stronger than ever.

At the university, Mariamne Whatley taught the course that was my academic introduction to women's health. Gabi and Biddy mothered me and encouraged me to go to medical school.

Thankfully, Kate Bowland was looking for a midwifery apprentice just as I became interested in attending home births. To anyone to whom I imparted knowledge of midwifery in abortion care, thanks are due to Kate and the other Santa Cruz midwives who I worked with, including Julie, Karen, Robin, and Roxanne.

Thank you to Marcia and Paul, the owners of my favorite pastry shop, who offered me a part-time job until I landed at Women's Health Care Services.

Sadly, I cannot thank Dr. Tiller, but I can thank his wife, Jeanne, and daughters Jennifer, Rebecca, and Krista. Even before my time at WHCS, Jim McMahon introduced me to a different way of providing abortion care. Much love to his wife, Gale, and his family, who continue to provide services in Los Angeles. I continue to appreciate Curtis Boyd and Glenna Halvorson-Boyd for giving Susan Robinson and me the opportunity to incorporate a third-trimester abortion practice into their Albuquerque clinic. And without Susan, none of the years in Albuquerque would have been possible. I am incredibly grateful for our friendship and collaboration.

I was fortunate to work with incredible staff in both Kansas and New Mexico. What was it that Dr. Tiller said? "There is no 'I' in TEAM." So true. In Kansas, I especially thank Cathy Reavis and JoAn Armentrout, who died before she could vote in the November election. Thank you for your commitment and dedication to this work that is so challenging and also so rewarding. I hope that our time together helped lay the groundwork for all the great accomplishments that lie in your future. I'm speaking to all of you in New Mexico, including Aíne, Alex, Andrea, Carla, Dan, Duda, Emily, Italia, Jazlyn, Jess, Joan, Maria, Michelle, Molly Mae, Monica, Nurse Molly, Sandra, Steve, Sue C., Susana, and Thaymi. To my midwifery colleagues at SWO, Kalin and Skye, thank you for keeping the midwifery spirit alive in our practice.

An incalculable amount of thanks to all the patients I cared for. You taught me so much about determination and bravery in the face of many obstacles. And thank you to Carly, Erika, and Garin for sharing your experiences as patients with me.

Years ago, Johanna Schoen invited me to speak about viability on a NAF panel and that got me thinking about this concept, which is a cornerstone of my book. And she was an early supporter of *Beyond Limits*. Very early on in the writing process, Carole Joffe gave me wise advice, which was to "just write." I cited Diana Greene Foster's groundbreaking work, *The Turnaway Study*, multiple times in *Beyond Limits*, but until now, I didn't mention how kind and supportive she was to me during my writing process. Thank you to Khiara Bridges, Katrina Kimport, and Gretchen Sisson, whose research informed my work.

There are an untold number of friends and colleagues, beyond the professionals, who helped with different iterations of the manuscript. Victoria and Helene were the first to hear a few excerpts that I read aloud to them in a motel outside Yosemite, and eventually, they also read the completed manuscript. As longtime academics, they well knew how arduous the process of writing is but they kept that to themselves and kept smiling and encouraging me.

Many readers offered incisive critiques and encouragement. They included Diana Greene Foster and Martha Shane, who read the proposal; Skye Bookless, Khiara Bridges, Kristen Jozkowski, Barbara Rhine, and Katie Watson, who read specific chapters; Lyn Barraza, Ellen Bernstein of the Wagettes, Rachel Levy, and Susan

Robinson, who read the completed manuscript; Chaya, Judith, Katie, Kelly, NoahLani, and Roni, who workshopped the book's title.

It would be untrue to say that writing this book was an unending joyful experience. At one point, Lana Wilson responded to my urgent call when I was in writing despair and gently walked me off the ledge. I thank my friends in my different worlds who hung in there with me including Ellen and Jill.

Bouldering at the Berkeley Ironworks climbing gym was always a great release from the written words on a screen. My amazing climbing instructor, Jeffrey, probably now knows more than he ever thought he would about abortion, specifically third-trimester care. Much appreciation to him, Ben, Lyn, Michelle, and Ryan Moon, who usually takes climbing photos but agreed to take my author photo. Thanks also to my climbing buddies, including Grace, Jenny, Khai, Mel, Quyen, and Sky.

The book was written under the backdrop of two losses. In October 2022, Carmen Landau, my mentee, close friend, and colleague, died unexpectedly. She continues to be in my thoughts and in my dreams.

The last part of the book was written during the Israeli invasion into Gaza. The unfolding devastation and horror make it hard to visualize a world where women can ever attain bodily autonomy and where children can enter a world where they and their families can live in safety and with adequate resources. Nevertheless, I hold on to a dream of limitless possibilities for all.

Finally, I will end where I began, with deep love and admiration for Julie and NoahLani.

NOTES

AUTHOR'S NOTE

1. A variation of the quote at the beginning of chapter 5 can be found in Carole Joffe, *Doctors of Conscience: The Struggle to Provide Abortion Before and After Roe V. Wade* (Boston: Beacon Press, 1995), 179.

INTRODUCTION

1. A term pregnancy lasts thirty-seven to forty weeks and is divided into trimesters. The first trimester is defined as the period of pregnancy up to twelve to fourteen weeks gestational age; the second trimester is between the end of the first trimester up to twenty-four to twenty-six weeks gestational age; and the third trimester is the period after twenty-four to twenty-six weeks. First-trimester abortions are performed one of two ways: utilizing a two-medication regimen for pregnancies up to eleven weeks, or through a five-to-seven-minute in-clinic aspiration. Depending on the gestational age, second-trimester abortions occur over one to two days, with medication given to prepare the cervix before extracting the fetus. There are variations in technique for third-trimester abortions, but my practice is the premature delivery of a stillborn, inducing fetal demise; preparing the cervix over one to two days; and then inducing labor on the second or third day.

2. According to the CDC (Katherine Kortsmit et al., "Abortion Surveillance—United States, 2021," *Morbidity and Mortality Weekly Report* 72, no. 9 [November 24, 2023]: 1–29, https://www.cdc.gov/mmwr/volumes/72/ss/ss7209a1.htm), of the 625,978 abortions performed in 2021, 93.5 percent were performed at thirteen weeks or earlier, 5.7 percent were performed at fourteen to twenty weeks, and 0.9 percent were performed at twenty-one weeks or later. There is not a further breakdown on the numbers that occur at twenty-four weeks and later, but given the paucity of clinics that perform third-trimester abortions, one can assume that the majority of post-twenty-one-week abortions occur between twenty-one and twenty-four weeks.

3. "For the stage subsequent to viability, the State in promoting its interest in the potentiality of human life may, if it chooses, regulate, and even proscribe, abortion except where it is necessary, in appropriate

medical judgment, for the preservation of the life or health of the mother."
Roe v. Wade, 410 U.S. 113, 93 S. Ct. 705, 35 L. Ed. 2d. 147 (1973).

4. Roe v. Wade, 410 U.S. 113, 93 S. Ct. 705, 35 L. Ed. 2d 147 (1973).
This sentence was footnoted in the decision (footnotes 59 and 60) with two
obstetrics textbooks: Jack A. Pritchard, Louis M. Hellman, and Ralph
Wynn, *Williams' Obstetrics*, 14th ed. (London: Butterworths, 1971), 493;
Dorland's Illustrated Medical Dictionary, 24th ed. (Philadelphia: W. B.
Saunders, 1965), 1,689.

5. Planned Parenthood of Central Missouri v. Danforth, 428 U.S. 52,
96 S. Ct. 2831, 49 L. Ed. 2d 788 (1976).

6. For another critique of common notions of viability, see Katrina
Kimport and Tracy Weitz, "Regulating Abortion Later in Pregnancy:
Fetal-Centric Laws and the Erasure of Women's Subjectivity," *Journal of
Health Politics, Policy, and Law* (August 2024), https://doi.org/10.1215
/03616878-11516772.

7. Diana Greene Foster, *The Turnaway Study: Ten Years, a Thousand
Women, and the Consequences of Having—or Being Denied—an Abortion*
(New York: Scribner, 2020).

CHAPTER 1: TUESDAY MORNING, FETAL INDICATIONS

1. Molly A. Minnick, Kathleen J. Delp, and Mary C. Ciotti, *A Time to
Decide, a Time to Heal: For Parents Making Difficult Decisions About Babies
They Love* (St. Johns, MI: Pineapple Press, 1992).

CHAPTER 2: NEW YORK

1. Since *Roe* was overturned, there has been a resurgence of interest in
the Del-Em. An anonymously authored instruction manual can even be
purchased titled *How to Get Your Period: A Guide to Performing Menstrual
Extraction* and published by Microcosm Publishing.

CHAPTER 3: TUESDAY MORNING, MATERNAL INDICATIONS

1. Medication abortions now comprise the majority of abortions performed in the United States. Highly effective at least up to eleven weeks,
the procedure consists of a regimen of two medications: mifepristone, an
anti-progesterone that stops the pregnancy from growing, and misoprostol, which causes uterine contractions that expel the pregnancy. Note that
both medications are also used at later gestational ages. There, mifepristone is used to help soften the cervix. Misoprostol is used to induce labor
both for pregnancy terminations and, at much lower doses, to induce
labor for live births.

CHAPTER 4: CALIFORNIA

1. An instrumented first-trimester abortion, distinct from a medication
abortion, typically takes five to seven minutes. A speculum is inserted and

the cervix is numbed with a local anesthetic. Dilators are inserted through the cervix, widening it enough so a cannula, a tube-like instrument, can be inserted into the uterus. Suction is applied and the uterus is emptied of its contents.

2. The D&X procedure was later demonized by the anti-abortion movement and renamed a "partial-birth abortion." In 2007, the Supreme Court upheld a federal ban and banned the procedure, without exception. In a prescient comment at the time, Representative Jerry Nadler of New York stated: "We can no longer rely on the Supreme Court to protect a woman's constitutional right to choose." Janice Hopkins Tanne, "US Supreme Court Approves Ban on 'Partial Birth Abortion,'" *The BMJ* 334, no. 7599 (April 28, 2007): 866–67, https://doi.org/10.1136/bmj.39192.397338.DB.

CHAPTER 5: TUESDAY AFTERNOON

1. I draw my answer about fetal pain from conclusions reached in the report by the Royal College of Obstetrics and Gynaecologists, *Fetal Awareness: Updated Review of Research and Recommendations for Practice*, originally reported in 2010, updated in December 2022, https://www.rcog.org.uk/media/gdtnncdk/rcog-fetal-awareness-evidence-review-dec-2022.pdf; and Susan J. Lee et al., "Fetal Pain: A Systematic Multidisciplinary Review of the Evidence," *JAMA* 294, no. 8 (August 2005): 947–54, https://doi/org/10.1001/jama.294.8.947.

CHAPTER 6: KANSAS

1. Promotional brochure, Women's Health Care Services, Wichita, Kansas, 2002, in author's possession.

2. AbortionDocs.org, "Need for Investigation of Shelley Sella, MD, George R. Tiller, MD, and Women's Health Care Services in the Abortion of Michelle Armesto (Berge)," January 2012, https://abortiondocs.org/wp-content/uploads/2012/01/Armesto-Complaint-Narrative.pdf.

CHAPTER 10: NEW MEXICO

1. Kathleen Sebelius went on to become Secretary of Health and Human Services in the Obama administration. Her term was cut short by the initially unsuccessful rollout of the Affordable Care Act.

CHAPTER 11: FRIDAY

1. This is in contrast to the findings of Gretchen Sisson, who studies the experiences of birth mothers who relinquish their babies for adoption. "When I asked mothers if they regretted their adoptions, many of them said they did unequivocally. This pattern is consistent with a survey of birth mothers that found that nearly half of them regretted their decision. However, even among mothers who wouldn't precisely say they regretted their adoption, it was rarely because they were clearly happy with their

relinquishment or believed it had been the best possible outcome. For these mothers, a lack of regret was rooted in their capacity to forgive themselves and acknowledge that they did the best they could at the time." Gretchen Sisson, *Relinquished: The Politics of Adoption and the Privilege of American Motherhood* (New York: St. Martin's Press, 2024), 174.

CHAPTER 12: BEYOND FRIDAY

1. Carly Grant, phone interview with author, March 27, 2024.

CHAPTER 13: FETAL INDICATIONS

1. Roosa Tikkanen et al., "Maternal Mortality and Maternity Care in the United States Compared to 10 Other Developed Countries," The Commonwealth Fund, issue brief 10 (November 18, 2020): 1–17, https://www.commonwealthfund.org/publications/issue-briefs/2020/nov/maternal -mortality-maternity-care-us-compared-10-countries.

2. Tikkanen et al., "Maternal Mortality and Maternity Care in the United States Compared to 10 Other Developed Countries," 1–17.

3. Katherine Kortsmit et al., "Abortion Surveillance—United States, 2020," *Morbidity and Mortality Weekly Report* 71, no. 10 (Summer 2022): 1–27, table 15, http://dx.doi.org/10.15585/mmwr.ss7110a1.

4. Shockingly, in 2021 the overall maternal mortality rate in the US was 32.9 deaths per 100,000 live births and 69.9 per 100,000 for Black women. Donna L. Hoyert, "Maternal Mortality Rates in the United States, 2021," National Center for Health Statistics E-Stats, 2023, https://www.cdc.gov /nchs/data/hestat/maternal-mortality/2021/maternal-mortality-rates -2021.htm.

5. NMRCRC has changed its name to Faith Roots Reproductive Action.

6. Erika Christensen and Garin Marschall, Zoom interview with author, August 26, 2023.

7. The National Women's Law Center reports that thirty-one states have laws permitting forced sterilization. National Women's Law Center, *Forced Sterilization of Disabled People in the United States*, 2021, https://nwlc .org/wp-content/uploads/2022/01/f.NWLC_SterilizationReport_2021 .pdf, accessed June 12, 2024.

8. According to the Guttmacher Institute, as of August 2023, eleven states ban abortions for reason of sex selection, five for reasons of race, eight for when the fetus may have a genetic anomaly. Three mandate counseling on perinatal hospice services before a patient can have an abortion for a lethal anomaly. One state, Kansas, requires this counseling before *any* abortion can be performed. Guttmacher Institute, "State Laws and Policies: Abortion Bans in Cases of Sex or Race Selection or Genetic Anomaly," August 31, 2023, https://www.guttmacher.org/state-policy/explore /abortion-bans-cases-sex-or-race-selection-or-genetic-anomaly. For important context, see Khiara M. Bridges, "The Dysgenic State: Environ-

mental Injustice and Disability-Selective Abortion Bans," *California Law Review* 110 (April 2022): 297–369, https://doi.org/10.15779/Z38P843X00.

9. Neelam Bohra, "Disabled Texans Face More Barriers to Accessing Abortion," *Texas Tribune*, February 20, 2024, https://www.texastribune.org/2024/02/20/texas-abortion-disabled/.

CHAPTER 14: MATERNAL INDICATIONS

1. Only Arkansas, Mississippi, and Alabama have higher rates than Louisiana. All four are in the South; all are red states. "Maternal Deaths and Mortality Rates," National Vital Statistics System, https://www.cdc.gov/nchs/maternal-mortality/mmr-2018-2021-state-data.pdf.

2. Guttmacher Institute, "State Laws and Policies: Counseling and Waiting Periods for Abortion," August 30, 2023, https://www.guttmacher.org/state-policy/explore/counseling-and-waiting-periods-abortion.

3. "Parents are entitled to a total of 12 months' leave in connection with a birth. These 12 months include the mother's entitlement of up to 12 weeks' leave during the pregnancy and 6 weeks' leave which can only be taken by the mother after the birth. In addition to these 12 months, each of the parents is entitled to 1 year's leave each, for each birth. This leave must be taken immediately after the first year of leave." Arbeidstilsynet.no, Norwegian Labour Inspection Authority, "Parental Leave," https://www.arbeidstilsynet.no/en/working-conditions/permisjoner/parental-leave/, accessed June 12, 2024.

4. The last complete breakdown of patients' economic status was in 2014. Three-fourths of abortion patients were low income: 49 percent living at less than the federal poverty level, and 26 percent living at 100–199 percent of the poverty level. Jenna Jerman, Rachel K. Jones, and Tsuyoshi Onda, *Characteristics of U.S. Abortion Patients in 2014 and Changes Since 2008* (New York: Guttmacher Institute, 2016), https://www.guttmacher.org/report/characteristics-us-abortion-patients-2014.

5. Guttmacher Institute, "State Laws and Policies: Parental Involvement in Minors' Abortions," September 1, 2023, https://www.guttmacher.org/state-policy/explore/parental-involvement-minors-abortions.

6. Now that Texas has banned abortion, the organization focuses on assisting teens with travel and practical support to access an abortion out of state. Jane's Due Process, https://janesdueprocess.org, accessed June 12, 2024.

CHAPTER 15: ADOPTION AND SAFE HAVEN LAWS

1. Because the rates are so low, historically, abortion mortality rates have been calculated in five-year increments. The last mortality rate, 0.45/100,000 abortions, was calculated from the years 2013–2019, a seven-year period due to a continued decline in deaths. Katherine Kortsmit et al., "Abortion Surveillance—United States, 2021," *Morbidity and Mortality*

Weekly Report 72, no. 9 (November 24, 2023): 1–29. In 2019, the overall maternal mortality rate was 20.1 per 100,000 and 44.0 for Black women. Donna L. Hoyert, "Maternal Mortality Rates in the United States, 2019," National Center for Health Statistics Health E-Stats, April 2021, https://www.cdc.gov/nchs/data/hestat/maternal-mortality-2021/E-Stat-Maternal-Mortality-Rates-H.pdf.

2. While Diana Greene Foster was surprised by the low rate of adoption, Gretchen Sisson, a co-investigator whose work focuses on adoption, was surprised by the *high rate*, in contrast to the significantly lower rate, 0.5 percent, of all adoption in American births. "These seemingly contradictory interpretations reflect an underlying truth about adoption relinquishment: it remains a rare experience when compared to the relatively common experiences of parenting and abortion, but it becomes meaningfully more frequent when women's choices are constrained." Gretchen Sisson, *Relinquished: The Politics of Adoption and the Privilege of American Motherhood* (New York: St. Martin's Press, 2024), 60–61.

3. For a nuanced view of adoption, see Sisson, *Relinquished.*

4. "So it seems to me, seen in that light, both *Roe* and *Casey* emphasize the burdens of parenting, and insofar as you and many of your amici focus on the ways in which forced parenting, forced motherhood, would hinder women's access to the workplace and to equal opportunities, it's also focused on the consequences of parenting and the obligations of motherhood that flow from pregnancy. Why don't the safe haven laws take care of that problem?" Amy Coney Barrett, *Dobbs. V. Jackson Women's Health* (Supreme Court docket number 19-1392), oral argument audio, December 1, 2021, MP3 audio (0:59:00), and PDF transcript (p. 56), https://www.supremecourt.gov/oral_arguments/audio/2021/19-1392.

5. Lori Bruce, "Unmet Needs, Unwanted Persons: A Call for Expansion of Safe Haven Laws," *Hastings Center Report* 46, no. 5 (September/October 2016): 7–8, https://doi.org/10.1002/hast.609.

6. "Unfortunately, the passion with which SHL's (Safe Haven Laws) have been created has not been matched with a commensurate demonstration of their effectiveness" (546). Michelle Hammond, Monica K. Miller, and Timothy Griffin, "Safe Haven Laws as *Crime Control Theater*," *Child Abuse & Neglect* 34, no. 7 (July 2010): 545–52, https://doi.org/:10.1016/j.chiabu.2009.11.006.

7. Every few years, throughout my time practicing, another such story made headlines. Here are a few of these headlines, each followed by the first line from the article: Associated Press, "Not Guilty Plea in Sorority Baby Killing," *San Francisco Chronicle*, August 11, 2004: "A former student of California State University in Chico pleaded not guilty in Butte County Superior Court to charges in killing her newborn son in her sorority room"; Hurst Laviana, "Infant Found Dead in Reno County," *Wichita Eagle*,

March 15, 2006: "The Reno County Sheriff's Department Is Investigating the Death of a Newborn Whose Body Was Found in an Undisclosed Location West of Hutchinson"; Associated Press, "Texas: Schoolgirl Kills Baby, Police Say," *New York Times*, April 3, 2008: "A 14-year-old girl gave birth to a full-term baby in a bathroom at her Houston-area junior high school, then tried to flush it down the toilet, killing the infant, the police said."

CHAPTER 16: ENDINGS

1. Following Dr. Tiller's death in 2009, as mentioned in chapter 8, Dr. Carhart (who died in 2023) opened an all-trimester clinic in Maryland. Dr. Matt Reeves subsequently opened the DuPont Clinic in Washington, DC. Partners in Abortion Care opened in 2022 in College Park, Maryland, offering all-trimester care.

EPILOGUE

1. Apiary for Practical Support, "Find Your Local Practical Support Organization," https://apiaryps.org/pso-list, accessed June 12, 2024; National Network of Abortion Funds, https://abortionfunds.org, accessed June 12, 2024.

2. The memory of Savita Halappanavar in Ireland, who was seventeen weeks pregnant when she died of overwhelming sepsis after being denied an abortion while miscarrying, looms large over these cases. She was repeatedly denied care in the week that she was hospitalized because the fetal heartbeat was still present. Her death spurred the movement for legalization in Ireland that occurred in 2018. For a full recounting of her treatment, see L. Lewis Wall, "The Ghost of Savita Halappanavar Comes to America," *Obstetrics & Gynecology 140*, no. 5 (November 2022): 724–28, https://doi.org/10.1097/AOG.0000000000004979.

Josseli Barnica was seventeen weeks pregnant in Texas and miscarrying. Doctors deferred treating her appropriately with a D and C and waited forty hours, until there was no detectable heartbeat. She died of overwhelming sepsis three days later. Cassandra Jaramillo and Kavitha Surana, "A Woman Died After Being Told It Would Be a 'Crime' to Intervene in Her Miscarriage at a Texas Hospital," *ProPublica*, October 30, 2024, https://www.propublica.org/article/josseli-barnica-death-miscarriage-texas-abortion-ban.

Nevaeh Crain was six months pregnant in Texas when she died of overwhelming sepsis after being sent home from two ERs. She was finally admitted to a hospital from a third ER, critically ill, and even then, care was delayed while two ultrasounds were performed to confirm fetal demise. Lizzie Presser and Kavitha Surana, "A Pregnant Teenager Died After Trying to Get Care in Three Visits to Texas Emergency Rooms," *ProPublica*, November 1, 2024, https://www.propublica.org/article/nevaeh-crain-death-texas-abortion-ban-emtala.

Due to a six-week abortion ban in Georgia, Amber Nicole Thurman drove to North Carolina to obtain a medication abortion. She did not pass all the pregnancy tissue and had signs of an infection. She was seen at a hospital in Georgia, where medical treatment was started, but the key and appropriate treatment, a D and C, was withheld. Her condition declined rapidly. When she was finally taken to the operating room for treatment, she died on the table. Kavitha Surana, "Abortion Bans Have Delayed Emergency Medical Care. In Georgia, Experts Say This Mother's Death Was Preventable," *ProPublica*, September 16, 2024, https://www.propublica.org/article/georgia-abortion-ban-amber-thurman-death.

Unable to obtain an abortion in Georgia, Candi Miller ordered on-line medication abortion pills. Days after taking the pills, she had only incompletely passed the pregnancy and was in excruciating pain. Afraid to seek care, she died at home. Kavitha Surana, "Afraid to Seek Care Amid Georgia's Abortion Ban, She Stayed at Home and Died," *ProPublica*, September 18, 2024, https://www.propublica.org/article/candi-miller-abortion-ban-death-georgia.

Three out of these four Americans were women of color.

3. The overall maternal mortality rate in 2021 in the US was 32.9 deaths per 100,000 live births and 69.9 per 100,000 for Black women. Donna L. Hoyert, "Maternal Mortality Rates in the United States, 2021," National Center for Health Statistics E-Stats, 2023, https://www.cdc.gov/nchs/data/hestat/maternal-mortality/2021/maternal-mortality-rates-2021.htm.

4. Eleanor Klibanoff, "Kate Cox's Case Reveals How Far Texas Intends to Go to Enforce Abortion Laws," *Texas Tribune*, December 13, 2023, https://www.texastribune.org/2023/12/13/texas-abortion-lawsuit/.

5. Remy Tunim, "Grand Jury Declines to Indict Ohio Woman Who Miscarried at Home," *New York Times*, January 11, 2024, https://www.nytimes.com/2024/01/11/us/brittany-watts-ohio-miscarriage.html.

6. "Texas Supreme Court Rules Against Women Denied Abortion Care Despite DangerousPregnancy Complications," Center for Reproductive Rights, May 31, 2024, https://reproductiverights.org/zurawski-v-texas-ruling-texas-supreme-court/.

7. Daniel Grossman et al., *Care Post-*Roe*: Documenting Cases of Poor-Quality Care Since the* Dobbs *Decision*, Advancing New Standards in Reproductive Health (ANSIRH), University of California, San Francisco, May 2023, https://www.ansirh.org/sites/default/files/2023-05/Care%20Post-Roe%20Preliminary%20Findings.pdf.

8. For a detailed overview of this phenomenon, see Purvaja S. Kavattur et al., *The Rise of Pregnancy Criminalization: A Pregnancy Justice Report*, Pregnancy Justice, September 2023, https://www.pregnancyjusticeus.org/wp-content/uploads/2023/09/9-2023-Criminalization-report.pdf.

9. For a day-by-day recounting of these efforts, see Jessica Valenti's Substack, "Abortion, Every Day," https://jessica.substack.com.

10. Eleanor Clift, "Court's Contraception Ruling Is a Scary Sign of What May Come," *Daily Beast*, March 12, 2024, https://www.thedailybeast.com/courts-contraception-ruling-is-a-scary-sign-of-what-may-come.

11. Joshua Sharfstein, "The Alabama Supreme Court's Ruling on Frozen Embryos," Johns Hopkins Bloomberg School of Public Health, February 27, 2024, https://publichealth.jhu.edu/2024/the-alabama-supreme-courts-ruling-on-frozen-embryos.

12. Isaac Maddow-Zimet and Candace Gibson, "Despite Bans, Number of Abortions in the United States Increased in 2023," Guttmacher Institute, March 19, 2024, updated May 10, 2024, https://www.guttmacher.org/2024/03/despite-bans-number-abortions-united-states-increased-2023.

13. See Plan C, https://www.plancpills.org, for referrals for medication abortion pills in any state.

14. Megan Messerly and Jennifer Haberkorn, "Biden: 'I Will Restore *Roe v. Wade* as the Law of the Land Again," *Politico*, March 7, 2024, https://www.politico.com/live-updates/2024/03/07/biden-state-of-the-union-live/biden-i-will-restore-roe-v-wade-as-the-law-of-the-land-again-00145720.

15. Sister Song, "Reproductive Justice," https://www.sistersong.net/reproductive-justice, accessed June 12, 2024. For a full-bodied discussion of reproductive justice, see also Renee Bracey Sherman and Regina Mahone, *Liberating Abortion: Claiming Our History, Sharing Our Stories and Building the Reproductive Future We Deserve* (New York: HarperCollins Publishers, 2024).